Collins

KS2
Arithmetic
SATs Question Book

Katherine Pate

Contents

Addition and Subtraction

Multiplication and Division

Fractions, Decimals and Percentages

Square and Cube Numbers

- You will need a pen, pencil, ruler and eraser.

- You may not use a calculator to answer any of the questions.

- Show your working on the grids provided.

- Answers are worth 1 or 2 marks. Long multiplication and long division questions are worth 2 marks each. 2 marks are awarded for a correct answer; 1 mark may be awarded for showing the correct method.

- Where questions are expressed as fractions, the answers should be given as fractions. All other answers should be given as whole or decimal numbers.

- There are three progress tests throughout the book to allow you to practise the skills again. Record your results in the progress charts to identify what you are doing well in and what you can improve.

Acknowledgements

Every effort has been made to trace copyright holders and obtain their permission for the use of copyright material. The author and publisher will gladly receive information enabling them to rectify any error or omission in subsequent editions. All facts are correct at time of going to press.

Published by Collins
An imprint of HarperCollins*Publishers*
1 London Bridge Street
London SE1 9GF

HarperCollins*Publishers*
Macken House, 39/40 Mayor Street Upper,
Dublin 1, D01 C9W8, Ireland

© HarperCollins*Publishers* Limited 2020

ISBN 9780008201623

First published 2016
This edition published 2020

11

British Library Cataloguing in Publication Data.

A CIP record of this book is available from the British Library.

Commissioning Editor: Michelle l'Anson
Author: Katherine Pate
Project Management and Editorial: Louise Williams and Katie Galloway
Cover Design: Sarah Duxbury and Kevin Robbins
Inside Concept Design: Paul Oates and Ian Wrigley
Text Design and Layout: Contentra Technologies
Production: Karen Nulty
Printed in India by Multivista Global Pvt. Ltd.

MIX
Paper | Supporting responsible forestry
FSC™ C007454

This book is produced from independently certified FSC™ paper to ensure responsible forest management.

For more information visit:
www.harpercollins.co.uk/green

1 392 + 4 =

1 mark

2 165 + 9 =

1 mark

3 142 + 10 =

1 mark

4 ☐ = 20 + 234

1 mark

5 196 + 30 =

1 mark

6 45 + 241 =

1 mark

7   316 + 25 =

1 mark

8   200 + 546 =

1 mark

9   112 + 550 =

1 mark

10   463 + 208 =

1 mark

11   197 + 306 =

1 mark

12   ☐ = 239 + 785

1 mark

Adding Whole Numbers

13 $4,213 + 25 =$

1 mark

14 $3,512 + 146 =$

1 mark

15 $5,243 + 1,426 =$

1 mark

16 $84 + 3,816 =$

1 mark

17 $2,916 + 1,302 =$

1 mark

18 $1,725 + 2,317 =$

1 mark

19 8,426 + 5,312 =

1 mark

20 ☐ = 4,713 + 6,208

1 mark

21 25,314 + 2,136 =

1 mark

22 13,813 + 231,104 =

1 mark

23 32,358 + 14,824 =

1 mark

24 535,126 + 57,819 =

1 mark

Total marks .... /24   How am I doing? 😊 😐 😣

Subtracting Whole Numbers

1   327 – 5 =

1 mark

2   451 – 7 =

1 mark

3   678 – 50 =

1 mark

4   264 – 23 =

1 mark

5 $\boxed{}$ = 352 – 36

1 mark

6   549 – 106 =

1 mark

7   541 − 215 =

1 mark

8   463 − 182 =

1 mark

9   791 − 308 =

1 mark

10   ☐ = 900 − 237

1 mark

11   821 − 546 =

1 mark

12   374 − 286 =

1 mark

Subtracting Whole Numbers

13 2,486 – 30 =

1 mark

14 5,327 – 200 =

1 mark

15 4,536 – 28 =

1 mark

16 6,249 – 120 =

1 mark

17 8,365 – 272 =

1 mark

18 ☐ = 7,148 – 339

1 mark

19   9,534 – 2,013 =

1 mark

20   3,148 – 1,926 =

1 mark

21   5,461 – 3,283 =

1 mark

22   30,000 – 2,200 =

1 mark

23   57,862 – 3,271 =

1 mark

24   343,215 – 16,413 =

1 mark

Total marks .... /24   How am I doing?

Multiplying Whole Numbers

1 41 × 2 =

1 mark

2 32 × 3 =

1 mark

3 15 × 4 =

1 mark

4 23 × 5 =

1 mark

5 52 × 6 =

1 mark

6 27 × 9 =

1 mark

7 9 × 40 =

1 mark

8 20 × 30 =

1 mark

9 2 × 3 × 5 =

1 mark

10 2 × 5 × 10 =

1 mark

11 43 × 100 =

1 mark

12 100 × 217 =

1 mark

Multiplying Whole Numbers

13 132 × 2 =

1 mark

14 206 × 3 =

1 mark

15 312 × 5 =

1 mark

16 2,123 × 3 =

1 mark

17 6,304 × 2 =

1 mark

18 4,020 × 5 =

1 mark

Total marks .... /18   How am I doing?

1

```
      4 2
  ×   1 3
```

2 marks

2

```
      3 1
  ×   2 3
```

2 marks

3

```
      2 5
  ×   1 6
```

2 marks

4

```
      3 6
  ×   4 3
```

2 marks

5

```
    1 2 4
  ×   2 1
```

2 marks

6

```
    3 6 4
  ×   1 9
```

2 marks

15

Long Multiplication

7

```
      4 1 3
  ×     3 5
```

	2 marks

8

```
      5 2 6
  ×     7 3
```

	2 marks

9

```
      8 1 7
  ×     5 4
```

	2 marks

10

```
    1 4 2 8
  ×     1 2
```

	2 marks

11

```
    3 0 4 1
  ×     3 2
```

	2 marks

12

```
    5 7 1 3
  ×     2 5
```

	2 marks

16 | Total marks .... /24 | How am I doing?

1 32 ÷ 8 =

1 mark

2 72 ÷ 6 =

1 mark

3 56 ÷ 7 =

1 mark

4 96 ÷ 8 =

1 mark

5 63 ÷ 3 =

1 mark

6 85 ÷ 5 =

1 mark

Dividing Whole Numbers

7   132 ÷ 12 =

1 mark

8   480 ÷ 6 =

1 mark

9   3,600 ÷ 9 =

1 mark

10   720 ÷ 1 =

1 mark

11   8,400 ÷ 7 =

1 mark

12   5,500 ÷ 11 =

1 mark

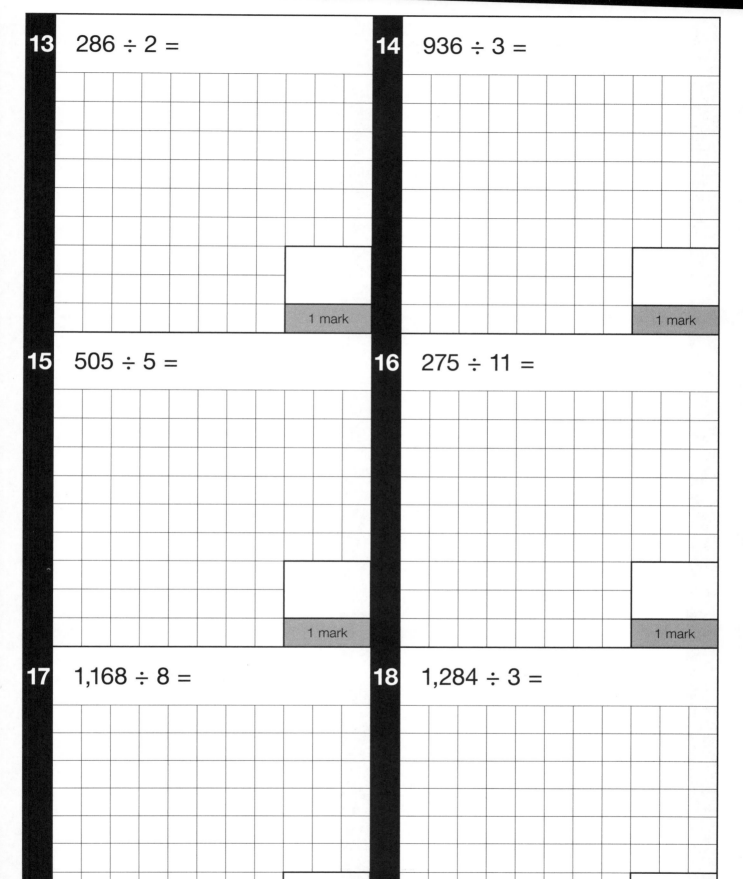

13 $286 \div 2 =$

1 mark

14 $936 \div 3 =$

1 mark

15 $505 \div 5 =$

1 mark

16 $275 \div 11 =$

1 mark

17 $1,168 \div 8 =$

1 mark

18 $1,284 \div 3 =$

1 mark

Total marks .... /18   How am I doing?   **19**

Long Division

1   1 3 | 1 5 6

2 marks

2   2 3 | 4 8 3

2 marks

3   1 7 | 4 0 8

2 marks

4   3 2 | 8 6 4

2 marks

5   1 5 | 3 0 4 5

2 marks

6   2 1 | 8 4 4 2

2 marks

7 1 4 | 3 1 2 2

2 marks

8 1 9 | 2 3 1 8

2 marks

9 2 2 | 5 3 0 2

2 marks

10 1 6 | 1 2 0 0

2 marks

11 1 8 | 1 1 1 6

2 marks

12 2 6 | 9 2 8 2

2 marks

1 581 + 7 =

1 mark

2 459 – 6 =

1 mark

3 34 × 2 =

1 mark

4 309 + 24 =

1 mark

5 45 ÷ 9 =

1 mark

6 384 – 60 =

1 mark

7 528 + 173 =

1 mark

8 3 × 2 × 7 =

1 mark

9 928 − 341 =

1 mark

10 ☐ = 2,417 + 6,823

1 mark

11 270 ÷ 3 =

1 mark

12 7,261 − 842 =

1 mark

Progress Test 1

13 4,800 ÷ 12 =

1 mark

14 17,294 + 6,431 =

1 mark

15 413 × 5 =

1 mark

16 6,241 − 3,829 =

1 mark

17 1,648 ÷ 4 =

1 mark

18 738,250 − 4,624 =

1 mark

19 5,216 × 3 =

1 mark

20 3,246 ÷ 6 =

1 mark

21

$$\begin{array}{r} 2\ 8 \\ \times\ \ 1\ 4 \\ \hline \end{array}$$

2 marks

22

$$\begin{array}{r} 2\ 1\ 4\ 5 \\ \times\ \ \ \ \ \ 3\ 4 \\ \hline \end{array}$$

2 marks

23 1 4) 4 2 7 0

2 marks

24 2 3) 1 5 4 1

2 marks

Total marks .... /28   How am I doing? 😊 😐 😖   25

1 $\dfrac{2}{5} + \dfrac{1}{5} =$

1 mark

2 $\dfrac{5}{9} - \dfrac{4}{9} =$

1 mark

3 $\dfrac{1}{8} + \dfrac{3}{8} =$

1 mark

4 $\dfrac{7}{8} - \dfrac{1}{8} =$

1 mark

5 $\dfrac{3}{4} + \dfrac{2}{4} =$

1 mark

6 $\dfrac{4}{5} + \dfrac{3}{5} =$

1 mark

7 $\frac{1}{2} + \frac{1}{4} =$

1 mark

8 $\frac{5}{8} - \frac{1}{4} =$

1 mark

9 $\frac{1}{5} + \frac{3}{10} =$

1 mark

10 $\frac{5}{6} - \frac{2}{3} =$

1 mark

11 $\frac{1}{3} + \frac{1}{12} =$

1 mark

12 $\frac{2}{5} + \frac{2}{15} =$

1 mark

13 $\dfrac{1}{5} + \dfrac{1}{2} =$

1 mark

14 $\dfrac{1}{4} + \dfrac{1}{6} =$

1 mark

15 $\dfrac{2}{3} - \dfrac{1}{8} =$

1 mark

16 $\dfrac{3}{5} - \dfrac{1}{4} =$

1 mark

17 $\dfrac{3}{4} + \dfrac{2}{7} =$

1 mark

18 $\dfrac{2}{3} + \dfrac{4}{5} =$

1 mark

Answers

Where answers are worth two marks, award TWO marks for the correct answer. If the answer is incorrect, award ONE mark for the formal method of long multiplication/long division with no more than ONE arithmetical error.

Question	Requirement	Marks
Pages 4–7 Adding Whole Numbers		
1	396	1
2	174	1
3	152	1
4	254	1
5	226	1
6	286	1
7	341	1
8	746	1
9	662	1
10	671	1
11	503	1
12	1,024	1
13	4,238	1
14	3,658	1
15	6,669	1
16	3,900	1
17	4,218	1
18	4,042	1
19	13,738	1
20	10,921	1
21	27,450	1
22	244,917	1
23	47,182	1
24	592,945	1
Pages 8–11 Subtracting Whole Numbers		
1	322	1
2	444	1
3	628	1
4	241	1
5	316	1

Question	Requirement	Marks
6	443	1
7	326	1
8	281	1
9	483	1
10	663	1
11	275	1
12	88	1
13	2,456	1
14	5,127	1
15	4,508	1
16	6,129	1
17	8,093	1
18	6,809	1
19	7,521	1
20	1,222	1
21	2,178	1
22	27,800	1
23	54,591	1
24	326,802	1
Pages 12–14 Multiplying Whole Numbers		
1	82	1
2	96	1
3	60	1
4	115	1
5	312	1
6	243	1
7	360	1
8	600	1
9	30	1
10	100	1
11	4,300	1

Answers

Question	Requirement	Marks
12	21,700	1
13	264	1
14	618	1
15	1,560	1
16	6,369	1
17	12,608	1
18	20,100	1
Pages 15–16 Long Multiplication		
1	546	2
2	713	2
3	400	2
4	1,548	2
5	2,604	2
6	6,916	2
7	14,455	2
8	38,398	2
9	44,118	2
10	17,136	2
11	97,312	2
12	142,825	2
Pages 17–19 Dividing Whole Numbers		
1	4	1
2	12	1
3	8	1
4	12	1
5	21	1
6	17	1
7	11	1
8	80	1
9	400	1
10	720	1
11	1,200	1
12	500	1

Question	Requirement	Marks
13	143	1
14	312	1
15	101	1
16	25	1
17	146	1
18	428	1
Pages 20–21 Long Division		
1	12	2
2	21	2
3	24	2
4	27	2
5	203	2
6	402	2
7	223	2
8	122	2
9	241	2
10	75	2
11	62	2
12	357	2
Pages 22–25 Progress Test 1		
1	588	1
2	453	1
3	68	1
4	333	1
5	5	1
6	324	1
7	701	1
8	42	1
9	587	1
10	9,240	1
11	90	1
12	6,419	1
13	400	1

Question	Requirement	Marks
14	23,725	1
15	2,065	1
16	2,412	1
17	412	1
18	733,626	1
19	15,648	1
20	541	1
21	392	2
22	72,930	2
23	305	2
24	67	2
Pages 26–29 Adding and Subtracting Fractions		
1	$\frac{3}{5}$	1
2	$\frac{1}{9}$	1
3	$\frac{4}{8} = \frac{1}{2}$	1
4	$\frac{6}{8} = \frac{3}{4}$	1
5	$\frac{5}{4} = 1\frac{1}{4}$	1
6	$\frac{7}{5} = 1\frac{2}{5}$	1
7	$\frac{3}{4}$	1
8	$\frac{3}{8}$	1
9	$\frac{5}{10} = \frac{1}{2}$	1
10	$\frac{1}{6}$	1
11	$\frac{5}{12}$	1
12	$\frac{8}{15}$	1
13	$\frac{7}{10}$	1
14	$\frac{5}{12}$	1
15	$\frac{13}{24}$	1
16	$\frac{7}{20}$	1
17	$\frac{29}{28} = 1\frac{1}{28}$	1
18	$\frac{22}{15} = 1\frac{7}{15}$	1
19	$\frac{11}{8} = 1\frac{3}{8}$	1
20	$\frac{23}{12} = 1\frac{11}{12}$	1

Question	Requirement	Marks
21	$5\frac{3}{5}$	1
22	3	1
23	$\frac{91}{15} = 6\frac{1}{15}$	1
24	$\frac{9}{10}$	1
Pages 30–32 Multiplying Fractions		
1	$\frac{2}{5}$	1
2	$\frac{3}{7}$	1
3	3	1
4	5	1
5	4	1
6	3	1
7	6	1
8	9	1
9	150	1
10	90	1
11	18	1
12	$22\frac{1}{2}$ or 22.5	1
13	$\frac{1}{6}$	1
14	$\frac{2}{10} = \frac{1}{5}$	1
15	$\frac{10}{21}$	1
16	$\frac{6}{40} = \frac{3}{20}$	1
17	$\frac{15}{24} = \frac{5}{8}$	1
18	$\frac{15}{60} = \frac{1}{4}$	1
Pages 33–34 Dividing Fractions		
1	$\frac{1}{6}$	1
2	$\frac{1}{20}$	1
3	$\frac{1}{16}$	1
4	$\frac{1}{15}$	1
5	$\frac{3}{10}$	1
6	$\frac{5}{18}$	1
7	$\frac{4}{36} = \frac{1}{9}$	1
8	$\frac{3}{15} = \frac{1}{5}$	1

Answers

Question	Requirement	Marks
9	$\frac{4}{10} = \frac{2}{5}$	1
10	$\frac{9}{30} = \frac{3}{10}$	1
11	$\frac{8}{36} = \frac{2}{9}$	1
12	$\frac{6}{21} = \frac{2}{7}$	1
Page 35 Adding and Subtracting Decimals		
1	6.4	1
2	1.87	1
3	2.36	1
4	22,626	1
5	2.92	1
6	253.11	1
Pages 36–37 Multiplying Decimals		
1	12	1
2	630	1
3	52.8	1
4	7,310	1
5	648.7	1
6	12,503	1
7	7	1
8	7.8	1
9	153	1
10	6.82	1
11	20.72	1
12	75.48	2
Pages 38–39 Dividing Decimals		
1	2.47	1
2	0.365	1
3	0.052	1
4	0.273	1
5	4.856	1
6	1.256	1
7	4.2	1

Question	Requirement	Marks
8	0.9	1
9	2.3	1
10	0.08	1
11	0.83	1
12	1.27	1
Page 40 Percentages		
1	3	1
2	5.6	1
3	21	1
4	75	1
5	80	1
6	60	1
Pages 41–44 Progress Test 2		
1	551	1
2	637	1
3	$\frac{5}{7}$	1
4	149,220	1
5	1.9	1
6	7.6	1
7	444	1
8	1.318	1
9	62,309	1
10	10	1
11	1,054	1
12	214	1
13	$\frac{1}{10}$	1
14	12.6	1
15	$\frac{2}{9}$	1
16	3	1
17	0.5	1
18	$\frac{3}{20}$	1
19	$\frac{60}{3} = 20$	1

Question	Requirement	Marks
20	$\frac{19}{40}$	1
21	$3\frac{7}{8}$	1
22	736	2
23	170	2
24	4,088	2
Page 45 Square and Cube Numbers		
1	9	1
2	8	1
3	1,001	1
4	46	1
5	104	1
6	9	1
Page 46 Place Value		
1	356	1
2	2,591	1
3	323,120	1
4	15,080	1
5	12,990	1
6	557,000	1
Pages 47–48 Negative Numbers		
1	−1	1
2	−4	1
3	−4	1
4	−8	1
5	−1	1
6	4	1
7	−3	1
8	2	1
9	−6	1
10	−3	1
11	−9	1
12	−4	1

Question	Requirement	Marks
Pages 49–51 Order of Operations		
1	4	1
2	5	1
3	42	1
4	80	1
5	13	1
6	22	1
7	6	1
8	7	1
9	28	1
10	25	1
11	5	1
12	9	1
13	17	1
14	24	1
15	16	1
16	12	1
17	22	1
18	27	1
Pages 52–56 Progress Test 3		
1	429	1
2	268	1
3	5.9	1
4	141	1
5	186	1
6	7	1
7	1,410	1
8	594	1
9	1,085	1
10	$\frac{6}{8} = \frac{3}{4}$	1
11	6	1
12	25,137	1

Answers

Question	Requirement	Marks
13	0.135	1
14	23	1
15	2.64	1
16	10.4	1
17	64	1
18	−4	1
19	3.8	1
20	$\frac{3}{6} = \frac{1}{2}$	1
21	1,042	1
22	0.08	1
23	28	1
24	$\frac{5}{24}$	1
25	$\frac{5}{8}$	1
26	12	1
27	$19\frac{1}{2}$ or 19.5	1
28	$\frac{20}{55} = \frac{4}{11}$	1
29	175,234	2
30	35	2

Progress Test 1

Q	Topic	✓ or X	See Page
1	Adding whole numbers		4
2	Subtracting whole numbers		8
3	Multiplying whole numbers		12
4	Adding whole numbers		5
5	Dividing whole numbers		17
6	Subtracting whole numbers		8
7	Adding whole numbers		5
8	Multiplying whole numbers		13
9	Subtracting whole numbers		9
10	Adding whole numbers		6
11	Dividing whole numbers		18
12	Subtracting whole numbers		10
13	Dividing whole numbers		18
14	Adding whole numbers		7
15	Multiplying whole numbers		14
16	Subtracting whole numbers		11
17	Dividing whole numbers		19
18	Subtracting whole numbers		11
19	Multiplying whole numbers		14
20	Dividing whole numbers		19
21	Long multiplication		15
22	Long multiplication		16
23	Long division		20
24	Long division		21

Progress Test 2

Q	Topic	✓ or X	See Page
1	Adding whole numbers		5
2	Multiplying decimals		36
3	Adding and subtracting fractions		26
4	Adding whole numbers		7
5	Percentages		40
6	Adding and subtracting decimals		35
7	Subtracting whole numbers		9
8	Dividing decimals		38
9	Subtracting whole numbers		11
10	Percentages		40
11	Multiplying whole numbers		14
12	Dividing whole numbers		18
13	Dividing fractions		33
14	Multiplying decimals		37
15	Dividing fractions		34
16	Multiplying fractions		30
17	Dividing decimals		39
18	Multiplying fractions		32
19	Multiplying fractions		31
20	Adding and subtracting fractions		28
21	Adding and subtracting fractions		29
22	Long multiplication		15
23	Long division		20
24	Long multiplication		16

Progress Test Charts

Progress Test 3

Q	Topic	✓ or ✗	See Page
1	Place value		46
2	Multiplying whole numbers		14
3	Adding and subtracting decimals		35
4	Multiplying whole numbers		12
5	Adding whole numbers		5
6	Dividing whole numbers		17
7	Adding whole numbers		6
8	Subtracting whole numbers		9
9	Multiplying whole numbers		14
10	Adding and subtracting fractions		26
11	Order of operations		50
12	Place value		46
13	Dividing decimals		38
14	Dividing whole numbers		17
15	Adding and subtracting decimals		35

Q	Topic	✓ or ✗	See Page
16	Multiplying decimals		37
17	Square and cube numbers		45
18	Negative numbers		47
19	Adding and subtracting decimals		35
20	Adding and subtracting fractions		27
21	Multiplying decimals		36
22	Dividing decimals		39
23	Dividing whole numbers		19
24	Dividing fractions		34
25	Adding and subtracting fractions		29
26	Percentages		40
27	Multiplying fractions		31
28	Multiplying fractions		32
29	Long multiplication		16
30	Long division		20

What am I doing well in?

_____

_____

_____

_____

What do I need to improve?

_____

_____

_____

19 $1\frac{5}{8} - \frac{1}{4} =$

1 mark

20 $2\frac{3}{4} - \frac{5}{6} =$

1 mark

21 $2\frac{1}{5} + 3\frac{2}{5} =$

1 mark

22 $1\frac{1}{7} + 1\frac{6}{7} =$

1 mark

23 $2\frac{2}{3} + 3\frac{2}{5} =$

1 mark

24 $2\frac{1}{5} - 1\frac{3}{10} =$

1 mark

Total marks .... /24   How am I doing?   29

Multiplying Fractions

1 $2 \times \dfrac{1}{5} =$

1 mark

2 $\dfrac{1}{7} \times 3 =$

1 mark

3 $4 \times \dfrac{3}{4} =$

1 mark

4 $\dfrac{5}{6} \times 6 =$

1 mark

5 $8 \times \dfrac{1}{2} =$

1 mark

6 $\dfrac{1}{3} \times 9 =$

1 mark

7 $\frac{3}{5} \times 10 =$

1 mark

8 $12 \times \frac{3}{4} =$

1 mark

9 $180 \times \frac{5}{6} =$

1 mark

10 $\frac{3}{8} \times 240 =$

1 mark

11 $1\frac{1}{2} \times 12 =$

1 mark

12 $15 \times 1\frac{1}{2} =$

1 mark

Multiplying Fractions

13 $\frac{1}{2} \times \frac{1}{3} =$

1 mark

14 $\frac{2}{5} \times \frac{1}{2} =$

1 mark

15 $\frac{5}{7} \times \frac{2}{3} =$

1 mark

16 $\frac{3}{8} \times \frac{2}{5} =$

1 mark

17 $\frac{3}{4} \times \frac{5}{6} =$

1 mark

18 $\frac{3}{5} \times \frac{5}{12} =$

1 mark

Total marks .... /18

How am I doing?

1 $\frac{1}{2} \div 3 =$

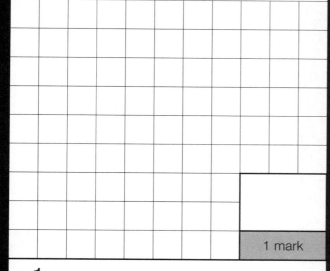

1 mark

2 $\frac{1}{4} \div 5 =$

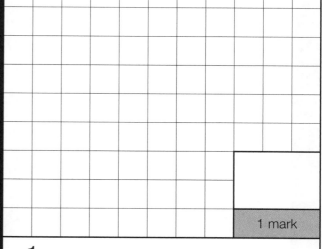

1 mark

3 $\frac{1}{8} \div 2 =$

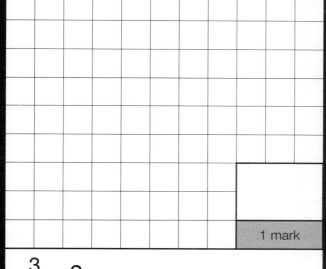

1 mark

4 $\frac{1}{5} \div 3 =$

1 mark

5 $\frac{3}{5} \div 2 =$

6 $\frac{5}{6} \div 3 =$

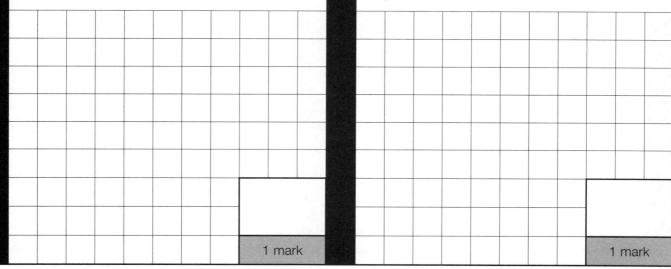

1 mark

1 mark

33

Dividing Fractions

7 $\frac{4}{9} \div 4 =$

1 mark

8 $\frac{3}{5} \div 3 =$

1 mark

9 $\frac{4}{5} \div 2 =$

1 mark

10 $\frac{9}{10} \div 3 =$

1 mark

11 $\frac{8}{9} \div 4 =$

1 mark

12 $\frac{6}{7} \div 3 =$

1 mark

34 Total marks .... /12   How am I doing? 😊 😐 😣

1 6.9 – 0.5 =

1 mark

2 0.05 + 1.82 =

1 mark

3 2.3 + 0.06 =

1 mark

4 13.21 + 9.416 =

1 mark

5 9 – 6.08 =

1 mark

6 268.31 – 15.2 =

1 mark

Total marks .... /6   How am I doing?   35

Multiplying Decimals

1   1.2 × 10 =

1 mark

2   6.3 × 100 =

1 mark

3   5.28 × 10 =

1 mark

4   7.31 × 1000 =

1 mark

5   6.487 × 100 =

1 mark

6   12.503 × 1000 =

1 mark

7 1.4 × 5 =

1 mark

8 2.6 × 3 =

1 mark

9 5.1 × 30 =

1 mark

10 3.41 × 2 =

1 mark

11 5.18 × 4 =

1 mark

12 6.29 × 12 =

2 marks

Total marks .... /13   How am I doing?   37

Dividing Decimals

1   24.7 ÷ 10 =

1 mark

2   36.5 ÷ 100 =

1 mark

3   5.2 ÷ 100 =

1 mark

4   27.3 ÷ 100 =

1 mark

5   485.6 ÷ 100 =

1 mark

6   1256 ÷ 1000 =

1 mark

7 8.4 ÷ 2 =

1 mark

8 3.6 ÷ 4 =

1 mark

9 6.9 ÷ 3 =

1 mark

10 0.72 ÷ 9 =

1 mark

11 2.49 ÷ 3 =

1 mark

12 6.35 ÷ 5 =

1 mark

Total marks .... /12   How am I doing? 😊 😐 😖

Percentages

1 10% of 30 =

1 mark

2 10% of 56 =

1 mark

3 50% of 42 =

1 mark

4 25% of 300 =

1 mark

5 20% of 400 =

1 mark

6 5% of 1200 =

1 mark

40

Total marks .... /6

How am I doing?

1 317 + 234 =

1 mark

2 6.37 × 100 =

1 mark

3 $\frac{2}{7} + \frac{3}{7} =$

1 mark

4 145,316 + 3,904 =

1 mark

5 10% of 19 =

1 mark

6 7.1 + 0.5 =

1 mark

7   700 – 256 =

1 mark

8   13.18 ÷ 10 =

1 mark

9   63,217 – 908 =

1 mark

10   50% of 20 =

1 mark

11   527 × 2 =

1 mark

12   856 ÷ 4 =

1 mark

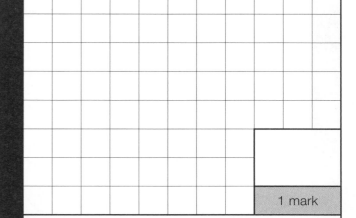

13 $\frac{1}{5} \div 2 =$

1 mark

14 $4.2 \times 3 =$

1 mark

15 $\frac{4}{9} \div 2 =$

1 mark

16 $\frac{1}{8} \times 24 =$

1 mark

17 $4.5 \div 9 =$

1 mark

18 $\frac{3}{5} \times \frac{1}{4} =$

1 mark

19 $\frac{2}{3} \times 30 =$

1 mark

20 $\frac{7}{8} - \frac{2}{5} =$

1 mark

21 $1\frac{5}{8} + 2\frac{1}{4} =$

1 mark

22

$$\begin{array}{r} 2\ 3 \\ \times \quad 3\ 2 \\ \hline \end{array}$$

2 marks

23

$$19 \overline{\smash{\big)}\,3\ 2\ 3\ 0}$$

2 marks

24

$$\begin{array}{r} 1\ 4\ 6 \\ \times \qquad 2\ 8 \\ \hline \end{array}$$

2 marks

Total marks .... /27

How am I doing?

1 $3^2 =$

| 1 mark |

2 $2^3 =$

| 1 mark |

3 $10^3 + 1 =$

| 1 mark |

4 $6^2 + 10 =$

| 1 mark |

5 $2^2 + 10^2 =$

| 1 mark |

6 $5^2 - 4^2 =$

| 1 mark |

Total marks .... /6   How am I doing?   **45**

Place Value

1   346 + 10 =

1 mark

2   2,491 + 100 =

1 mark

3   324,120 – 1000 =

1 mark

4   15,180 – 100 =

1 mark

5   13,000 – 10 =

1 mark

6   547,000 + 10,000 =

1 mark

Total marks .... /6

How am I doing?

1   0 − 1 =

1 mark

2   −3 − 1 =

1 mark

3   −5 + 1 =

1 mark

4   −7 − 1 =

1 mark

5   2 − 3 =

1 mark

6   −1 + 5 =

1 mark

7 1 − 4 =

1 mark

8 −2 + 4 =

1 mark

9 −4 − 2 =

1 mark

10 −8 + 5 =

1 mark

11 −2 − 7 =

1 mark

12 5 − 9 =

1 mark

Total marks .... /12

How am I doing?

1   3 + 2 – 1 =

1 mark

2   10 – 7 + 2 =

1 mark

3   2 × 3 × 7 =

1 mark

4   5 × 8 × 2 =

1 mark

5   5 × 2 + 3 =

1 mark

6   4 + 3 × 6 =

1 mark

Order of Operations

7 12 − 2 × 3 =

1 mark

8 15 − 4 × 2 =

1 mark

9 6 × 8 − 20 =

1 mark

10 9 × 3 − 2 =

1 mark

11 10 ÷ 5 + 3 =

1 mark

12 6 + 12 ÷ 4 =

1 mark

13 20 − 18 ÷ 6 =

1 mark

14 32 − 24 ÷ 3 =

1 mark

15 8 × 6 ÷ 3 =

1 mark

16 54 ÷ 9 × 2 =

1 mark

17 3 × 4 + 2 × 5 =

1 mark

18 6 × 8 − 3 × 7 =

1 mark

Total marks .... /18   How am I doing?   51

1 419 + 10 =

1 mark

2 134 × 2 =

1 mark

3 5.1 + 0.8 =

1 mark

4 47 × 3 =

1 mark

5 27 + 159 =

1 mark

6 63 ÷ 9 =

1 mark

7 1,024 + 386 =

1 mark

8 800 − 206 =

1 mark

9 217 × 5 =

1 mark

10 $\frac{1}{8} + \frac{5}{8}$ =

1 mark

11 5 × 2 − 4 =

1 mark

12 26,137 − 1000 =

1 mark

13 $13.5 \div 100 =$

1 mark

14 $92 \div 4 =$

1 mark

15 $2.6 + 0.04 =$

1 mark

16 $1.3 \times 8 =$

1 mark

17 $8^2 =$

1 mark

18 $3 - 7 =$

1 mark

19 8 − 4.2 =

1 mark

20 $\frac{1}{3}$ + $\frac{1}{6}$ =

1 mark

21 1.042 × 1000 =

1 mark

22 0.56 ÷ 7 =

1 mark

23 308 ÷ 11 =

1 mark

24 $\frac{5}{8}$ ÷ 3 =

1 mark

25 $1\frac{3}{8} - \frac{3}{4} =$

1 mark

26 15% of 80 =

1 mark

27 $1\frac{1}{2} \times 13 =$

1 mark

28 $\frac{2}{5} \times \frac{10}{11} =$

1 mark

29

```
    2 1 3 7
  ×     8 2
  ─────────
```

2 marks

30

```
1 8 | 6 3 0
```

2 marks

Total marks .... /32

How am I doing?

CHANGING BRITAIN

THE RISE OF WOMEN

B E T T Y   W I L L I A M S

Can Democracy Work for Women?

B.T. Batsford Ltd · London

First published 1994

© Betty Williams 1994

All rights reserved. No part of this
publication may be reproduced in any
form or by any means, without permission
from the Publisher.

Typeset by Goodfellow & Egan Ltd,
Cambridge

and printed in Singapore

Published by
B.T. Batsford Ltd
4 Fitzhardinge Street
London W1H 0AH

A catalogue record for this book is
available from the British Library

ISBN 0 7134 7015 1

British Coinage before Decimalization

Until 1970, when decimal currency was adopted, the pound
was divided into shillings. There were twenty shillings to the
pound and twelve pence to the shilling.

old money	abbreviation	value in new pence*
one penny	1d	less than ½p
sixpence	6d	2½p
half a crown	2s 6d or 2/6d	12½p
ten shillings	10s or 10/-	50p

* Remember that prices are now higher than in the past
because of inflation.

Over the last 150 years the position of women in our society has changed beyond measure. Today we talk about citizens' rights and we automatically expect women to have the same rights as men, but when Queen Victoria came to the throne in 1837 one-half of the population – the female half – had very few rights at all.

No women had the vote and no woman could become an MP. Women could not take part in local government, and could not sit on a jury, let alone be a magistrate or judge. They could not go to university; secondary education was almost non-existent for them. Though a number of women were journalists, writers and primary-school teachers, they were barred from other professions. They could not, for example, become doctors, lawyers or civil servants.

Married women had even fewer rights than those who were single. In his *Commentary on the Laws of England* Sir William Blackstone stated: 'By marriage the very being or legal existence of a woman is suspended, or at least it is incorporated or consolidated into that of the husband, under whose wing, protection and cover she performs everything, and she is therefore called in our law a *femme covert*.' Blackstone was writing in 1765 yet by 1850 the position, with the one exception of infant custody, was still the same. In law a married woman's property, including personal belongings such as jewellery, was owned by her husband, whether she had inherited it, bought it herself or received it as a gift. If she worked, any money she earned belonged to her husband even if the couple were separated. Divorce was virtually impossible.

Long before our story begins, some women had started to fight against these injustices. The Women's Movement was certainly not something that began with the feminists – the 'women's libbers' – of the 1960s. It has its roots as far back as the seventeenth century when a woman called Aphra Behn was ridiculed as a 'petticoat author' for daring to protest in her plays and novels at the inferior status of women.

A little later an unsuccessful campaign for a women's college was started by another pioneer, Mary Astell. She outlined her plans in a booklet called *A Serious Proposal to the Ladies by a Lover of Her Sex*, published in 1694, but failed to get enough financial support.

At the end of the eighteenth century Mary Wollstonecraft wrote what many regard as the first feminist tract. Her *Vindication of the Rights of Woman* (1792) argued for equality of the sexes in terms of education, work and politics. Wollstonecraft was attacked not only for her radical views but also for her unconventional lifestyle. She had several love affairs and, though unmarried, gave birth to a child. She later married the radical philosopher William Godwin.

Women took an active part in the Chartist movement of the 1830s, demanding votes for all adults, but the campaign petered out and the cry for women's suffrage was not taken up again until the 1860s. In the first half of the nineteenth century, the feminist movement was mainly concerned with gaining legal rights over property and children, and one of the leading figures in this struggle was Caroline Norton.

When she separated from her husband in 1836, Norton found that in law he owned her property, was entitled to her earnings as a writer, and was the sole legal guardian of their children: she had no rights of custody or even access. George Norton, a lawyer and MP, was a drunkard who attacked and beat his wife during their frequent quarrels. When she left him he banished their three young children to Scotland and refused to let her see them. Her protests against this situation, which she declared was 'an injustice not to be borne', were partially vindicated when a Custody of Infants Act was passed by Parliament in 1839. It gave the mother the right of custody of children under the age of seven if the courts agreed she was 'of good character'.

In many ways Caroline Norton is an unsung heroine of the women's rights movement; few people today have even heard of her. Yet her personal battles in the nineteenth century were important because she notched up the first victory in a fight which was to be waged by many different women – and men – on many different fronts, well into the twentieth century.

Victorian ladies sewing. 'Accomplishments' such as embroidery formed a large part of the education of middle-class girls in the nineteenth century.

Mid-Victorian Britain was a society shot through with contradictions. Great industries and clever inventions generated immense wealth and power, yet the labouring classes lived in sordid conditions and terrible poverty. A powerful woman was on the throne, yet the status of her female subjects was as low as it had ever been. In a dispute with her husband over her earnings, Caroline Norton was applauded by spectators when she exclaimed in court: 'I do not ask for my rights. I have no rights; I have only wrongs.'

'I have no rights; I have only wrongs'

In the 1850s the fight against the wrongs of married women was taken up by another strenuous campaigner, Barbara Bodichon. She was married to a French surgeon named Eugène Bodichon, who, unlike George Norton, shared his wife's advanced views and was happy for her to carry on her campaign in England. As the daughter of the radical MP Benjamin Leigh-Smith, Barbara Bodichon had been well educated. She attended Bedford College, one of two colleges of further education for women founded in London in the 1840s. Her physical appearance was also striking. The woman novelist George Eliot, who was a friend and fellow-campaigner, called her 'noble-looking Barbara' and took her as the model for the heroine of her novel *Romola*. The two women were among the founders of the *English Woman's Journal*, which became the mouthpiece of the women's rights movement. The offices of the *Journal* were in Langham Place in London and its contributors, scathingly referred to by critics as 'The Ladies of Langham Place', wrote on a wide range of issues from women's employment rights and higher education to the plight of governesses.

In 1854 Barbara Bodichon published a pamphlet entitled *A Brief Summary in Plain Language, of the Most Important Laws Concerning Women*, setting out the ways in which the English legal system discriminated against married women: 'We do not say that these laws of property are the only unjust laws concerning women . . . but they form a simple, tangible, and not offensive point of attack.' Her first move was to launch a petition demanding rights for married women, including the right to own property and to keep their earnings. It was signed by 26,000 people and was presented to both Houses of Parliament.

Some of the proposals in the petition were eventually incorporated into the Matrimonial Causes Act of 1857, which was primarily concerned with divorce law. Until then it had only been possible to get a divorce by private Act of Parliament, but the new Act allowed divorce through the courts. However, although a man could divorce his wife for adultery, a woman had to prove in addition that her husband had committed incest, or was guilty of cruelty or desertion. As a concession to the Bodichon proposals, which had already been debated favourably in Parliament, the 1857 Act laid down that a married woman could inherit and bequeath property, and that a wife separated from her husband could keep her own earnings.

Despite opposition from many influential people, including Queen Victoria, the fight for women's rights continued and in 1870 another success was achieved with the Married Woman's Property Act, which allowed married women living with their husbands to keep their earnings. A second Custody of Infants Act was passed in 1877, giving the custody of children up to the age of sixteen to the mother. The father still remained the sole legal guardian, however, and it was not until 1925 that this situation was changed. In 1882 another milestone was reached with the passing of an act giving married women the same rights over property as single women.

Another 'point of attack' for women's rights campaigners in the mid-nineteenth century was education. While boys had traditionally been educated in prestigious public schools and in often equally long-established grammar schools, girls were thought to have neither the brains nor the stamina to benefit from much education at all.

Although working-class girls were in many cases able to attend government-aided elementary schools, middle- and upper-class girls were usually given the rudiments of learning at home by a governess or in small private schools. 'Accomplishments' such as embroidery, drawing and music were thought much more appropriate for females than academic study and were prized as social assets.

Two redoubtable women – Frances Buss and Dorothea Beale – became the pioneers of girls' secondary education in the nineteenth century. In 1850 Miss Buss founded the North London Collegiate School and in 1858 Miss Beale became the principal of Cheltenham Ladies' College. Both women held the startling belief that girls should have the same sort of education as boys, and both gave evidence to the Royal Commission, known as the Schools Inquiry, set up by the government to investigate secondary education. The Commission's report, published

A husband discovers that his wife has been unfaithful in this painting of 1858. What future would the woman have? What might happen to her children?

in 1868, found girls' schools 'inferior' to boys'. The report constituted a turning point in the education of women.

Among others who gave evidence to the Commission was Emily Davies, who had recently scored a success in her campaign for higher education for women. At that time women were still not admitted to any English universities, but in 1864 Davies had persuaded the Cambridge authorities to allow schoolgirls to take their Local Examination papers as an experiment. The Local, instituted in 1858, was a preliminary qualifying exam designed to ensure a minimum standard of education before the colleges picked their own

entrants. It was the first time that secondary-school girls had taken such an examination and in most subjects, especially English, they did well. Cambridge University agreed to allow girls to take the Local for a trial period of three years, although they had no hope of being admitted as under-graduates to the university. The decision was a victory for Davies, who totally rejected proposals that women should have separate universities and study for different exams from male students. Both she and Miss Buss felt that 'different' would mean 'lower'.

In 1869 Emily Davies founded a women's college at Benslow House, Hitchin, with the object of storming the bastion of Cambridge University, which was some twenty miles away. In 1872 three women sat the Cambridge Tripos (final examination) in Classics, and all passed. However, they were not awarded degrees – they

had only been allowed to sit the Tripos as a favour.

In 1873 Emily Davies moved the establishment to a village just outside Cambridge, where it became Girton College, which today is part of the university. Though eventually women undergraduates at Cambridge were allowed to attend the same lectures as the men, to sit the Tripos and be awarded 'degree certificates', it was not until 1947 that they were admitted as full members of the university.

In 1878, however, London University decided that 'every degree, honour and prize awarded by the University shall be accessible to students of both sexes on equal terms'. In 1879 two women's colleges were opened at Oxford University which, in 1919, admitted women to full membership with the right to take degrees on the same basis as men.

The Rights of Women

A woman of twenty-one becomes an independent creature . . . But if she unites herself to a man, the law immediately steps in, and she finds herself legislated for, and her condition of life suddenly and entirely changed . . . she loses her separate existence, and is merged in that of her husband.

It is always said, even by those who support the existing law, that it is in fact never acted upon by men of good feeling. That is true; but the very admission condemns the law, and it is not right that the good feeling of men should be all that a woman can look to for simple justice.

From A Brief Summary, in Plain Language, of the Most Important Laws Concerning Women *by Barbara Bodichon (1854)*

The Queen is most anxious to enlist every one who can speak or write to join in checking this mad, wicked folly of 'Women's Rights', with all its attendant horrors, on which her poor feeble sex is bent, forgetting every sense of womanly feeling and propriety . . . God created men and women different – then let them remain each in their own position.

Queen Victoria writing to Mr Martin, 29 May 1870. Quoted in Carol Bauer and Lawrence Ritt, Free and Ennobled, Source Readings in the Development of Victorian Feminism *(1979)*

Imagine you are a nineteenth-century husband; would you feel that 'the good feeling of men' was enough for a woman wanting justice? Why do you think Queen Victoria was so opposed to the campaign for women's rights?

Two students in the laboratory at Girton College, Cambridge, in 1877. Why was it unusual for young women to be conducting scientific experiments at this period?

A rather solemn bride and bridegroom, photographed at their wedding in 1863. Why do you think the bride was marrying someone so much older than herself? Was marriage preferable to spinsterhood in Victorian times?

The Equality of the Sexes

I would draw no line of demarcation, so as to limit the extent of knowledge which either boy or girl may acquire. I would throw open the portals of knowledge freely to both . . . The mind has properly no sex. It is the mind of a human being, and consequently there must be of necessity a similarity in the instruction of both sexes.

From The Education of Girls *by Frances Buss (1865), quoted in Dale Spender (ed.),* The Education Papers *(1987)*

Many, however, thought otherwise. George Romanes, a Cambridge naturalist and friend of Charles Darwin, wrote:

Seeing that the average brain-weight of women is about five ounces less than that of men, on merely anatomical grounds we should be prepared to expect a marked inferiority of intellectual power in the former.

From Mental Differences of Men and Women *by George J. Romanes (1887), quoted in Dale Spender (ed.),* The Education Papers *(1987)*

What do you think Miss Buss meant when she said that 'the mind has properly no sex'? Do you agree with her? Do you think George Romanes would approve of education in Britain today?

1 Imagine a confrontation between Frances Buss or Emily Davies and George Romanes. What would they say to each other? You might like to act out the scene in class.

2 Read the opening chapters of George Eliot's novel *Middlemarch*. What impressions do you form of the life of the heroine, Dorothea Brooke?

3 Arrange a school visit to Girton College, Cambridge, where there are many paintings of women pioneers. Emily Davies is commemorated in the college chapel.

4 You are the editor of a modern version of the *English Woman's Journal* (see p. 4). What issues of interest to women today would you feature in the magazine?

The life of Annie Besant, from her conventional marriage in 1867 to her later crusades in India, where many regarded her with reverence. Which scene depicts her campaigns in Britain? What do you think is the artist's attitude towards her?

In Victorian times birth-control methods were unknown in most homes. Contraceptives did exist and towards the end of the century some upper- and middle-class couples tried to limit the size of their families by the use of condoms. But little, if anything, was known about such matters by the mass of the population. Working-class women, with few means to support their children, had to cope with constant pregnancies. Families of ten or more were common, as were infant deaths, especially in the overcrowded slum areas of industrial towns.

Annie Besant, a socialist reformer and writer, determined to do something about this situation. She had scandalized Victorian society by daring to speak and write against social injustice. As a member of the National Secular Society, an organization which rejected the Christian Church, she believed everyone should be free to make up their own minds on topics of importance. She and her friends were castigated as 'Free Thinkers'.

In 1877 Annie Besant and Charles Bradlaugh, a radical MP, published a pamphlet called *The Fruits of Philosophy* by an American doctor, Charles Knowlton, which advocated birth control and described methods of contraception. They offered it for sale at 6d. (2½p.) – a price even most working women could afford – and 800 copies were sold on the first day. Besant and Bradlaugh were immediately arrested and put on trial for publishing material 'likely to deprave public morals'. They were sentenced to imprisonment but successfully appealed against the verdict. As a result of the case Besant, who was separated from her husband, lost the custody of her daughter.

Victorians faced another moral

dilemma in the form of prostitution. Though Queen Victoria had presented the nation with a picture of an idyllic home life in which the devoted mother and father were surrounded by loving children, the reality in many homes was quite different. A thin veneer of respectability covered the sexual activities of many upper- and middle-class men, who thought it natural that they should visit prostitutes while their wives, encouraged to be 'pure and innocent', languished idly at home. Estimates vary, but it is known that there were vast numbers of prostitutes in Victorian Britain. Some authorities put the figure at one in six of all unmarried women between the ages of fifteen and fifty. Police estimates were much lower. A heartening fact about the Victorian age, however, is that, downtrodden as much of the female population was, there was never a shortage of women of character and determination, ready to come forward to fight for their less-favoured sisters. The woman who attacked the double standard that made prostitutes into criminals, while letting the men who used them go unpunished, was Josephine Butler.

Wealthy and well-educated, she was the daughter of an enlightened Northumberland landowner and the wife of George Butler, an equally enlightened teacher and Principal of the Liverpool College for Boys. Her husband supported her in all her campaigns because, as she wrote in a memoir, 'the idea of justice to women, of equality between the sexes . . . seems to have been instinctive in him'. He also supported her when, stricken with grief after the death of their five-year-old daughter, she became a prison and workhouse visitor in an attempt to 'find some pain keener than my own'. Her

work among the poorest women in society led her to try to help the 'penny whores' on the quaysides and in the alleyways of Liverpool.

Annie Besant and her friends were castigated as 'Free Thinkers'

In 1864, 1866 and 1869, the three Contagious Diseases (CD) Acts were passed. These were part of a cleaning-up operation to improve the health of Britain's fighting men. Venereal disease was rife in both the army and navy, and the blame was put on prostitutes. Under the Acts, any woman suspected of being a prostitute – and this meant any woman over the age of twelve, which was then legally the age of consent to sexual intercourse – could be arrested and given an unpleasant and usually brutal internal examination to find out if she had venereal disease. If so, she was locked in a special hospital until she was declared 'clean'. If she refused to be examined, she was imprisoned without trial. Men, however, were not subject to arrest on suspicion of having the disease.

In 1869 Josephine Butler became head of a Ladies' National Association formed to fight for the repeal of the CD Acts. In the first year of the campaign she travelled nearly 4,000 miles around the country and spoke at ninety-nine meetings. A petition was signed by 2,000 women including Florence Nightingale and Harriet Martineau, a feminist writer and journalist who contributed a series of articles on the subject to the *Daily News*.

A system to regulate prostitution was in operation in France throughout the nineteenth

century and was copied in several other European countries. Prostitutes were registered by the police and lived in licensed houses (brothels), where they were subject to regular medical examinations. Among Josephine Butler's supporters was the French writer Victor Hugo, who wrote to her: 'I am with you to the fullest extent of my power . . . England prepares to adopt from France a detestable system, that, namely, of a police dealing with women as outlaws . . . The slavery of black women is abolished in America, but the slavery of white women continues in Europe; and laws are still made by men in order to tyrannise over women.'

In a pamphlet, *The Constitution Violated*, Butler argued that for the entire female population the Acts amounted to a suspension of habeas corpus, the cornerstone of British liberty, which forbids imprisonment without trial. She continually made the point that women were forced to go on the streets because they needed the money to live, not because they were wicked, and that for many it was prostitution or starvation.

She also attacked the widespread 'White Slave Traffic' in Victorian Britain, in which girls and young women were abducted and sold for prostitution abroad. With her help, the journalist W.T. Stead exposed the traffic in young girls for paedophiliac vice rings. In 1885 he wrote a sensational series of articles for the *Pall Mall Gazette*, of which he was editor. In the same year the age of consent was raised to sixteen, and in 1886, after seventeen years of ceaseless campaigning, Josephine Butler saw the CD Acts repealed.

‘An Awkward Encounter in Regent Street’. This cartoon appeared in a Victorian periodical, **The Day's Doings**, in 1870. ‘That girl seems to know you, George!’ says the man's wife. Who is the girl and how might the husband explain the meeting?

Controlling the Population

We republish this pamphlet, honestly believing that on all questions affecting the happiness of the people, whether they be theological, political or social, fullest right of free discussion ought to be maintained at all hazards . . .

We believe, with the Rev. Mr Malthus, that the population has a tendency to increase faster than the means of existence, and that *some* checks must therefore exercise control over population; the checks now exercised are semi-starvation, and preventable disease; the enormous mortality among the infants of the poor is one of the checks which now keeps down the population. The checks that ought to control population are scientific, and it is these which we advocate. We think it more moral to prevent the conception of children, than, after they are born, to murder them by want of food, air and clothing.

From the preface by Annie Besant and Charles Bradlaugh to The Fruits of Philosophy *by Charles Knowlton (1877)*

I say that this is a dirty, filthy book, and the test of it is that no human being would allow the book on his table, no decently educated English husband would allow even his wife to have it.

Sir Hardinge Gifford, the Solicitor General, counsel for the prosecution at the trial of Besant and Bradlaugh, 1877. Quoted in Olivia Bennett, Annie Besant *(1988)*

Do you agree that ‘scientific checks’ ought to be used to control the population? What do you consider to be the ideal size for a family?

Infant Mortality

Deaths of infants up to one year old, per 1,000 live births:

Year	England & Wales	Scotland
1870	160	123
1880	153	125
1890	151	131
1900	154	128
1910	105	108
1920	80	92
1930	60	83
1940	57	78
1950	30	39
1960	22	26
1970	18	19

Draw a graph to illustrate the trend of these figures. What does it show?

Figures from Abstract of British Historical Statistics *by B.R. Mitchell and P. Deane (1962) and* Second Abstract *by B.R. Mitchell and H.G. Jones (1971);* British Social Trends since 1900 *by A.H. Halsey (1988); and* Annual Abstract of Statistics, *HMSO (1993)*

1 Who was the Rev. Malthus referred to by Besant and Bradlaugh in their preface to Knowlton's pamphlet? Using a good encyclopaedia, find out about his theories concerning population control.

2 Imagine that you are a supporter of Josephine Butler. Write a speech for one of her protest meetings.

3 A contemporary view of Victorian prostitution is provided by investigator Bracebridge Hemyng in volume 4 of Henry Mayhew's famous book *London Labour and the London Poor* (1862). Extracts from this account can also be found in *London's Underworld* by Peter Quennell (Bracken Books, 1983).

4 What attempts are being made today to control the world's rising birth-rate? Find out about the work of the charity Population Control. You can contact them at:
231 Tottenham Court Road
London W1P 9AE

◄

Josephine Butler, philanthropist and champion of the downtrodden prostitute. What was her main achievement in the field of women's rights?

Class divisions were rigorously defined in the nineteenth century, but all classes of women had one thing in common: the jobs available to them were severely restricted.

For many working-class women the only option was domestic service. By the 1890s one out of every three unmarried women in Britain was 'in service', most of them living as well as working in the houses of their employers. They slept in cold, sparsely furnished attic rooms and worked from early morning until late evening, cleaning, polishing and serving. Though they did get meals, pay was negligible and time-off scant.

With the growth of large department stores, another job – that of shop assistant – became available to working-class women. They too had to 'live in', usually in large dormitories in the stores' attics. Their lives were closely controlled and they often had to pay fines for misdemeanours such as being late, losing a duster or gossiping. Before the First World War they often worked for up to seventy-five hours a week for very low pay.

In the industrial towns women also found work in factories and mills. They were employed in large numbers in the textile mills of Lancashire and Yorkshire, in the Staffordshire potteries, and in the flax and jute industries of Dundee and Belfast. Most were paid about half the wage of a man in a similar job. In Lancashire school-leavers of both sexes went to work in the cotton mills. Many started there as 'half-timers' while still attending lessons, and often they worked in the card or carding room, preparing raw cotton for the

spinners. Here they risked contracting 'card-room asthma' (byssinosis), caused by the inhalation of fluff.

When working men began to organize themselves into trade unions to press for better pay and conditions, some women, especially those in the Lancashire cotton industry, joined too. The North-East Lancashire Amalgamated Society, for example, was formed in 1859 with a membership of both sexes.

Most women workers, however, had to struggle not only against their employers but also against the prejudice of male employees who feared that women would undercut their wages and take their jobs. Because of this the women's trade-union movement developed in most areas quite separately from that of the men. It was dominated by a number of forceful women, among them Emma Paterson.

A bookbinder by trade, Paterson founded the Women's Protective and Provident League, for bookbinders, upholstresses, shirt- and collar-makers, dressmakers and hat-makers, in 1874. A year later she won the right for women delegates to attend the Trades Union Congress, which had been formed by male unions in 1868 to determine a common policy. At Emma Paterson's death in 1886 her union, now called the Women's Trade Union League, comprised about thirty women's trade societies.

The Dinner Hour, Wigan *by Eyre Crowe. Why did so many nineteenth-century North-country women work in the textile mills? Was any alternative employment available?*

Two years later a strike for better pay and conditions by match-makers at Bryant and May's factory at Bow in east London caused a furore among liberal-minded people in Britain. The match girls worked long hours for low wages, out of which they had to pay numerous fines for 'misdeeds'. Their work was also extremely dangerous because the chemical phosphorus, into which the matches were dipped, caused a disease known as 'phossy jaw' (necrosis) which made the teeth, gums and jawbone rot away.

they risked contracting 'card-room asthma'

When Annie Besant wrote an article exposing this situation in a radical magazine called *The Link*, Bryant and May dismissed three of their workers for giving her information. Led by Besant, the 1,400 factory workers went on strike and, backed by left-wing sympathizers and liberal-minded people who attended protest meetings and contributed to a strike fund, they won their case.

The match girls' working conditions improved, the fines imposed on them were abolished and their wages raised slightly. The sacked workers were reinstated and Annie Besant became the first secretary of a newly formed Union of Women Match-makers. It was not until 1908, however, that the use of the type of phosphorus causing phossy jaw was banned in the manufacture of matches.

In 1906 Mary Macarthur, a Scottish trade unionist, founded the first general union for unskilled women employed in any industry, the National Federation of Women Workers. One of her greatest achievements was the exposure of the working conditions of women in the

'sweated trades', who spent long hours crammed into one-room 'sweatshops' in the East End of London and in other large cities. Macarthur also protested at the plight of those women who had to work at home, labouring for up to sixteen hours a day sewing garments, stitching gloves or pasting up boxes for starvation wages. Her Anti-Sweating League resulted in a Board of Trade inquiry and, in 1909, the setting up of Trade Boards (later known as Wages Councils) to fix minimum rates of pay.

The first four trades to have wages set by the Boards were chain-making, box-making, lace-making and the sewing of ready-made clothes. In the chain-making trade, where wages had been 4s. to 6s. a *week*, the new rate was 2½d. an *hour*, which averaged 10s. to 11s. for a 55-hour week.

Some employers would not pay the new rates. In 1910 the women chain-makers of Cradley Heath, Birmingham, went to the TUC conference carrying their chains. They asked the delegates to 'help us get 2½d. an hour for making these. We mean to fight for it.' The *Birmingham Post* reported that the TUC delegates shouted 'We will!'

Backed by Mary Macarthur, about five hundred women, some of them members of the Chain Makers' Association, which was part of the National Federation of Women Workers, went on strike for the new rates. The Federation agreed to give them strike pay of 4s. a week each, and about £4,000 was raised for this purpose in a country-wide campaign. The strike ended successfully after ten weeks with the employers agreeing to pay the new wages.

Wage Slaves

A typical case is that of a girl of 16, a piece-worker . . . [Her] splendid salary of 4s. [a week] is subject to deductions in the shape of fines; if the feet are dirty, or the ground under the bench is left untidy, a fine of 3d. is inflicted . . . in some departments a fine of 3d. is inflicted for talking. If a girl is late she is shut out for 'half the day' . . . and 5d. is deducted from her day's 8d. . . .

Such is a bald account of one form of white slavery as it exists in London . . . who cares for the fate of these white wage slaves? Born in slums, driven to work while still children, undersized because underfed, oppressed because helpless, flung aside as soon as worked out, who cares if they die or go on the streets, provided only that Bryant and May shareholders get their 23 per cent. . .?

From 'White Slavery in London' by Annie Besant, published in The Link, *23 June 1888*

What are the main points that Annie Besant is trying to get across in her article? Do you think she has succeeded? To what is she alluding when she calls the match girls' work 'white slavery'?

Women and Unions

So long as women are unprotected by any kind of combination . . . working men not unnaturally look with suspicion on their employment in trades in some branches of which men are engaged . . . At three successive annual congresses of . . . trades unions, the needs of women's unions have been brought before them and each time someone present has asserted that women *cannot* form unions. The only ground for this assertion appears to be that women *have not* yet formed unions.

From 'The Position of Working Women and How to Improve It' by Emma Paterson, published in Labour News, *1874*

As a nineteenth-century working man, what would have been your attitude to women employees? Would you have welcomed them into your union? Give your reasons.

This **Punch** *cartoon, entitled 'Needle Money', dates from the mid-nineteenth century and shows a home-worker desperately trying to finish her work. What do you understand by the term 'needle money'?*

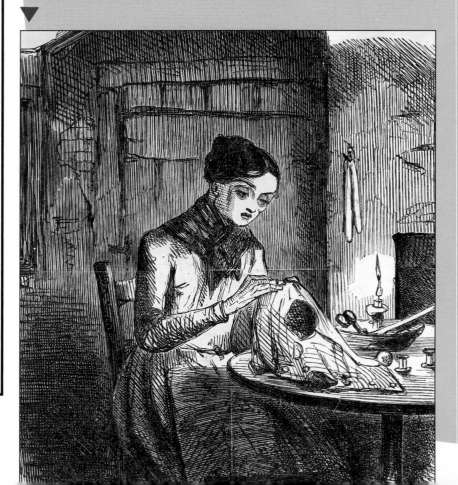

Women match-makers in the Bryant and May Factory at Bow, east London. What were the conditions that caused the match girls to go on strike in 1888?

◀

1 Write an account of a day in the life of a domestic servant. One book you might find helpful is *Not in Front of the Servants* (1972) by Frank Dawes.

2 Obtain a copy of the novel *North and South* by the nineteenth-century writer Elizabeth Gaskell from your school or public library. Chapter 13 contains an account of a visit by the heroine, Margaret Hale, to a dying mill girl, Bessy Higgins. Note Bessy's description of a carding room.

3 Can you find out if any women are still working in sweatshop conditions in Britain today? Ask your local library if it has any publications by the Low Pay Unit or write for information to the Unit at:
27 Amwell Street
London EC1R 1UN

4 The following museums show some of the work done by women in the nineteenth century: the Black Country Museum, Dudley; the Tonge Moor Textile Museum, Bolton; the Lewis Textile Museum, Blackburn; the Gladstone Pottery Museum, Longton, Staffs; the Ironbridge Gorge Museum, Telford; the National Museum of Labour History, Manchester.

In Service

Although most households employed only one or two domestic servants, grander establishments boasted dozens. Some of the different jobs undertaken by servants were listed, together with their average annual wages, in a government report of 1899.

Class of work, female	Average wage
Between-maid	£11
Scullerymaid	£13
Kitchenmaid	£14
Nurse–housemaid	£14 10s.
General servant	£13
Housemaid	£15 15s.
Nurse	£18 15s.
Parlourmaid	£19 10s.
Laundrymaid	£23
Cook	£20
Lady's maid	£25
Cook–housekeeper	£33
Housekeeper	£43 15s.
Class of work, male	
Boy	£11
Manservant (duties undefined)	£38 10s.
Footman	£26 10s.
Butler	£58 10s.

What does the above table tell you about the different roles of male and female domestic staff in a large house? What do you think a 'between-maid' was?

From Money Wages of Indoor Domestic Servants *(Cmnd 9346) by Miss Collett (1899)*

While working-class women *had* to work, both in the home and outside it, many upper- and middle-class females led a life of leisure – and often boredom. The maxim 'A woman's place is in the home' was accepted by most women as well as men, and the sole ambition of the great majority of single women in the nineteenth century was to catch a suitable husband. The numbers of young men in Britain, however, had been drastically reduced by wars, service in British territories overseas, and emigration. Inevitably there was a surplus of unmarried women, who were unfairly derided as 'old maids'.

If her father or brother could not support her, or died leaving her unprovided for, a spinster had little choice but to take on the lonely, poorly paid and often despised life of a governess to the children of her more fortunate contemporaries. This was the fate that befell Charlotte, Emily and Anne Brontë, the daughters of a clergyman from Haworth in West Yorkshire. Although the sisters were mostly unsuccessful as governesses, all three went on to become celebrated novelists, and Charlotte and Anne were able to use their teaching experiences in their novels.

The Victorian male's view of women as capricious beings who nevertheless performed the role of 'ministering angels' to the sick, probably made it inevitable that when women did strike out for the right to professional employment, the first area in which they succeeded was the 'caring' profession of nursing.

Until she was thirty Florence Nightingale, who loathed her luxurious, idle life, fought the opposition of her family to get some training as a nurse, which she eventually received at a religious community in Germany. When the Crimean War started in 1854, she persuaded the Secretary of State for War to allow her to take a party of nurses out to the military hospital at Scutari (present-day Üsküdar in Turkey). She was appalled by the conditions she found, but set about cleaning up the filth, dressing the men's wounds and introducing order and standards of hygiene. Resented at first by the male doctors and hospital orderlies, she soon earned the respect of the wounded soldiers and has been remembered ever since as the Lady with the Lamp.

Florence Nightingale's most important achievements, however, came after she returned to England, determined to make

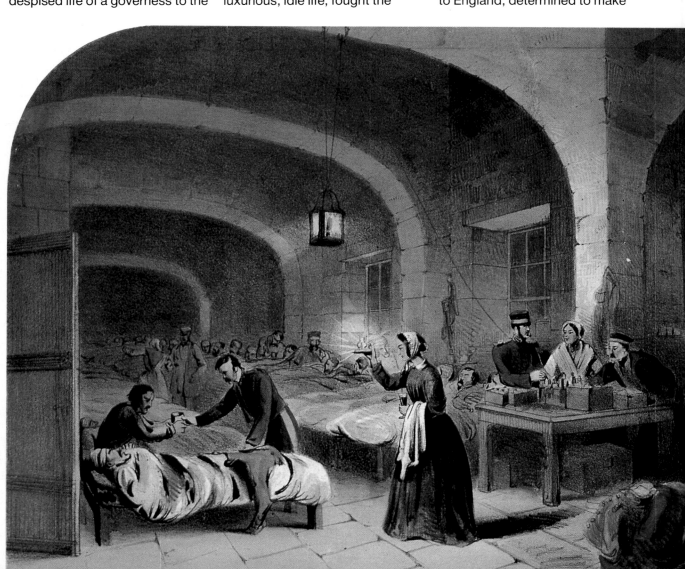

nursing into a profession with a proper training structure. In 1860 she helped to found the Nightingale School for nurses at St Thomas's Hospital in London. Only fifteen pupils enrolled in the first year but by the turn of the century Britain had 10,000 fully trained nurses and midwives.

Four years after Florence Nightingale went out to the Crimea, the first woman doctor was entered on the British Medical Register (list of qualified doctors). Her name was Elizabeth Blackwell. She had been born in Bristol in 1821 and, like many of the other feminist pioneers, was

Florence Nightingale visits wounded soldiers in the military hospital at Scutari. What does the picture show of the order and discipline she imposed on the wards?

lucky to have an enlightened father who gave his daughters the same opportunities as his sons. A sugar refiner, he emigrated with his family to America and it was in New York that Elizabeth was able to study medicine, qualifying in 1849. She gained hospital experience in Paris and in 1859 came to England to give a series of lectures.

One of these was attended by Elizabeth Garrett, daughter of a liberal-minded grain-merchant from Suffolk. She was so fired with enthusiasm that she decided not only to become a doctor herself but to fight for the right of *all* British women to study medicine.

The loophole that had enabled Elizabeth Blackwell to join the Medical Register was closed in 1860 when a new regulation decreed that only women with English medical degrees could be entered on it. However, no medical schools in England would admit women. Elizabeth Garrett got round this obstacle by watching operations as a student nurse, studying for a medical degree in Paris and then becoming a member of the Society of Apothecaries, which enabled her to open a women's dispensary in London. In 1871 she married James Anderson, who became a staunch ally in her fight for women's rights. In the same year she founded the New Hospital (later renamed the Elizabeth Garrett Anderson Hospital), which was staffed entirely by women for women patients.

In 1877, after some teaching hospitals in England had agreed to accept women medical students, another pioneer, Sophia Jex-Blake, opened her own

medical school for women in London. She later started a medical school and women's hospital in Edinburgh. By 1900 there were 200 women doctors but it was not until 1948 that it was made compulsory for all medical schools to admit female students on the same basis as men.

Among the jobs that had come to be considered respectable for women by the end of the nineteenth century was that of the secretary or office clerk. The invention of the typewriter and the telephone, and the development of shorthand brought about a revolution in office work, with female shorthand-typists supplanting male clerks, and telephone exchanges being staffed by women operators. The female typist working for a male boss became the norm in offices and even today secretarial work is still largely done by women.

In 1870, when the telegraph system passed into government control, the Post Office became the first civil-service department to take on women staff, and the rest of the civil service soon followed suit. Though female civil servants were well paid in comparison with other women workers, they were paid considerably less than men doing similar jobs, as were teachers, who comprised the largest category of professional women. An Equal Pay League was formed in 1904 by members of the National Union of Teachers, to which both sexes belonged. However, the League received little backing from the male-dominated union and in 1910 it broke away to become the National Union of Women Teachers.

She soon earned the respect of the wounded soldiers

Operators at a telephone exchange in the 1890s. The telephone system, which was run by the Post Office, was a new undertaking at the time. Why did it employ so many women?

The Governess

I said in my last letter that Mrs. —— did not know me. I now begin to find that she does not intend to know me; that she cares nothing about me, except to contrive how the greatest quantity of labour may be got out of me . . . I used to think that I should like to be in the stir of grand folks' society; but I have had enough of it – it is dreary work to look on and listen. I see more clearly than I have ever done before, that a private governess has no existence, is not considered as a living rational being, except as connected with the wearisome duties she has to fulfil.

Charlotte Brontë writing to her sister Emily, 8 June 1839. Quoted in Elizabeth Gaskell, The Life of Charlotte Brontë *(1857)*

Why were governesses despised and downtrodden? Why do you think the vast majority were spinsters?

At Scutari

On Thursday last we had 1,715 sick and wounded in this hospital (among whom 120 cholera patients) and 650 severely wounded . . . when a message came to me to prepare for 510 wounded . . . arriving from the dreadful affair of Balaclava . . . We had but half an hour's notice before they began landing the wounded. Between one and nine o'clock we had the mattresses stuffed, sewn up, laid down – alas! only on matting on the floor – the men washed and put to bed and all their wounds dressed . . . The operations all performed in the ward – no time to move them.

Would you rather have worked as a governess, like Charlotte Brontë, or with Florence Nightingale at Scutari? Why?

Letter from Florence Nightingale to Dr Bowman, a London surgeon, 14 November 1854. Quoted in Margaret Forster, Significant Sisters *(1984)*

Post Office Wages

When eighteen-year-old Frank Hopkin was promoted from Male Learner to Sorting Clerk and Telegraphist at Leeds Post Office in 1905, he copied out the pay scales for men and women and the minimum qualifications at each level.

Minimum Qualifications

Male
For 12s. a week

Female
For 10s. a week

Postal: Ability to sort 300 inward letters, or 300 letters primary sorting, in 12 minutes, mis-sorts not to exceed 12.

Telegraph: To send 20 and receive 12 words a minute on the instruments in use.

Male
For 14s. a week

Female
For 12s. a week

Postal: Expert in primary sorting, with a general knowledge of the rules governing the despatch and receipt of mails.

Telegraph: Ability to send and receive public messages.

Male
For 16s. a week.
19s. on attaining 19 years of age

Female
For 13s. 6d. a week.
16s. on attaining 19 years of age

Postal: Competency in General Sorting.
Telegraph: Ability to take sole charge of Morse and Double Plate Sounder Circuits.

If you had been a woman post-office worker in 1905, would you have thought the pay scales were fair? As a man in a similar job, would your opinion have remained the same?

From the private papers of Frank Melville Hopkin

Elizabeth Garrett Anderson faces a board of examiners in Paris in 1870. Why did she attend medical school in France rather than in England?

1 How many different teachers' unions are there? Ask your teacher for information about them. Are any of those to which teachers belonged at the turn of the century still in existence? If so, how have they changed?

2 Read chapters 2 and 3 of Anne Brontë's novel *Agnes Grey* (1847), which give a vivid picture of life as a governess in the nineteenth century.

3 Imagine that you were either one of the nurses at Scutari, or one of the wounded soldiers. Write an account of your life in the military hospital, giving your view of Florence Nightingale.

4 Sophia Jex-Blake wrote of 'the very widespread desire existing among women for the services of doctors of their own sex'. Do you agree with her that patients should have the right to choose to see a male or female doctor?

5 See if you can arrange a school visit to either the Brontë Parsonage Museum at Haworth, West Yorkshire, or the Florence Nightingale Museum, 2 Lambeth Palace Road, London SE1.

Women's suffrage became a burning crusade in the later years of the nineteenth century, when women began to campaign for the right to vote in elections. The first women's suffrage committee was founded by Barbara Bodichon in 1866 to press for the inclusion of women in the Second Reform Bill, which gave the vote to a million more men. Among its members were Elizabeth Garrett and Emily Davies. They collected nearly 1,500 signatures for a petition presented to Parliament by the radical philosopher and MP John Stuart Mill.

Mill was an ardent supporter of women's emancipation and when the Reform Bill was debated in the House of Commons he proposed an amendment that would allow some women the vote. It was defeated – but the fight was on. Suffrage committees sprang up in numerous cities. The movement was particularly strong in Lancashire, where the Manchester Society for Women's Suffrage was formed in 1867 (the year the Reform Bill was passed) by Lydia Becker. One of the leading suffragists in the early stages of the campaign, she edited the *Women's Suffrage Journal* for twenty years.

Since the Municipal Franchise Act of 1869, some women ratepayers had been able to vote in local government elections. From 1870 they were also allowed to vote in the election of school boards and to stand for membership of these. However, a third Reform Act, passed in 1884, again denied women the right to vote in general elections while extending the franchise to nearly two-thirds of the male population, including many working men. So what became known as The Cause went on, its supporters collecting signatures, presenting petitions, writing articles, making speeches and lobbying MPs. A large number of Liberal and radical MPs were by now in favour of votes for women and the suffrage case was regularly debated in Parliament.

. . . a tube was forced down the nose or mouth to the stomach

Elizabeth Garrett's younger sister Millicent made her first public speech for women's suffrage at a meeting in London in 1869. She had worked for The Cause from an early age and had married an MP, Henry Fawcett, who was also one of its supporters. Millicent Fawcett became President of the newly formed National Union of Women's Suffrage Societies (NUWSS), which brought all the suffragist organizations under one umbrella in 1897. It produced a newspaper called *The Common Cause*. Many of its branches in the north of England contained 'radical suffragists' who campaigned not just for women to have the vote on the same terms as men but for votes for all working-class women as well. By the turn of the century, with The Cause little further advanced, many of these radicals began to lose faith in Millicent Fawcett's methods of peaceful persuasion. A new mood – a militant one – was in the air and this was to change the face of the campaign in a dramatic way.

'Deeds not words' was the motto of the Women's Social and Political Union (WSPU), founded in Manchester in 1903 by Emmeline Pankhurst and her daughters Christabel and Sylvia. They pledged to fight for the immediate enfranchisement of women by means of what they called 'political action'. Peaceful methods of canvassing were rejected in favour of confrontation. The popular press dubbed the radicals 'suffragettes' in contrast to Millicent Fawcett's 'suffragists'.

The first big protest came in 1905 at a Liberal election meeting in Manchester. Christabel Pankhurst and Annie Kenney, a mill worker from Oldham, stood up and demanded, 'Will the Liberal Government give votes to women?' They refused to be silenced and in the end were thrown out of the meeting. Outside, still protesting, they were arrested. In court they refused to pay the fines imposed and were given prison sentences. Annie Kenney got three days for disorderly behaviour, and Christabel Pankhurst, who had committed the unladylike offence of spitting at a policeman, seven days.

So started the pattern of militant protest. Mrs Fawcett, while condemning violence, conceded that ' . . . militancy has been brought into existence by the blind blundering of politicians who have not understood the women's movement'. Members of the government, in common with many men, felt that women should be concerned only with domestic and social matters. They regarded women as too ignorant, emotional and irrational to play any part in affairs of state, especially foreign policy.

In 1906 the WSPU moved its headquarters to London, where two supporters, Emmeline and Frederick Pethick-Lawrence, published a weekly newspaper called *Votes for Women*. A third organization, the Women's Freedom League (WFL), was formed in 1907 by Charlotte Despard, a former member of the WSPU, who objected to its increasing militancy and nondemocratic structure.

Suffrage agitation increased in 1908 when Herbert Henry Asquith, an opponent of women's right to vote, became the new Liberal Prime Minister. Violence broke out at a demonstration outside Parliament and two suffragettes took a taxi to Downing Street, where they threw stones through the windows of No. 10. They and twenty-five other women were sent to prison.

As the protests increased, more and more women were gaoled. They retaliated by going on hunger strike. The authorities decided to feed them forcibly and brutal tactics were employed to do this. The prisoner was held down by wardresses and a tube forced down the nose or mouth to the stomach. Liquid food was poured in, usually causing the victim to vomit.

These tactics did nothing to quell the militants, however. In the course of their campaign they smashed thousands of windows, chained themselves to railings outside public buildings, set fire to pillar boxes, railway stations and empty houses, slashed paintings in art galleries, demolished three greenhouses in Kew Gardens and carried out a bombing campaign aimed at damaging buildings without harming anyone. The campaign united all classes of women in a way that would have seemed impossible in Victorian times. This alliance of titled ladies, professional women, middle-class housewives and working-class agitators such as the Lancashire mill girls rocked the foundations of Edwardian society, which was driven to extraordinary lengths to try to defeat it.

This dramatic poster, showing a suffragette being forcibly fed in prison, was used by the WSPU in its campaign for women's suffrage. Note the number of wardresses holding the prisoner down. Who is the poster intended to influence?

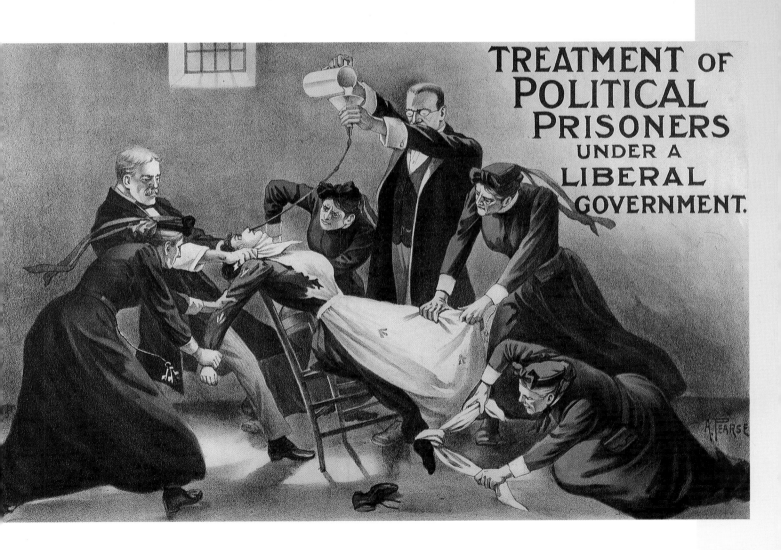

TREATMENT OF POLITICAL PRISONERS UNDER A LIBERAL GOVERNMENT.

Opponents of The Cause

Some women, however, did not want the vote:

We believe that the emancipating process has now reached the limits fixed by the physical constitution of women, and by the fundamental difference which must always exist between their main occupations and those of men. The care of the sick and the insane; the treatment of the poor; the education of children; in all these matters, and others besides, they have made good their claim to larger and more extended powers. We rejoice in it. But when it comes to questions of foreign or colonial policy, or of grave constitutional changes, then we maintain that the necessary and normal experience of women . . . does not and can never provide them with such materials for sound judgment as are open to men . . . the pursuit of a mere outward equality with men is for women not only vain but demoralising.

From An Appeal against Female Suffrage, *a petition presented to Parliament by the Women's Anti-Suffrage League (1889)*

How far had nineteenth-century women 'extended' their 'powers' in the occupations listed in the petition? Do you agree that men are better qualified than women to determine government policy?

A suffragette is arrested by three policemen, while a fourth watches from his horse. Why did some women reject peaceful persuasion and take more radical action in their campaign for the vote?

The scene outside Swan & Edgar's department store in Piccadilly Circus, London, after an attack by suffragettes. How effective do you think this campaign was? What would have been the reaction of the shop-owners?

SWAN & EDGA

A Plea for Women's Suffrage

It will surely not be denied that women have, and ought to have, opinions of their own on subjects of public interest, and on the events which arise as the world wends its way. But if it be granted that women may, without offence, hold political opinions, on what ground can the right be withheld of giving the same expression of effect to their opinions as that enjoyed by their male neighbours? . . . to individual women the law says: '. . . we will tax your property and earnings as we see fit, but in return . . . you shall not possess the minutist fraction of personal political power; we will not allow you to have the smallest share in the government of the country of which you are a denizen, nor any voice in the making of the laws which determine the legal and political status of persons of your sex.'

Now can any man who feels that he would not like to be addressed in language of this sort, seriously believe that women do like it?

Do you think Lydia Becker puts a good case for female suffrage? What are the main points she makes?

From an article by Lydia Becker in support of John Stuart Mill's amendment to the Second Reform Bill, published in the Contemporary Review, *March 1867*

1 **Stage a class debate between suffragists and anti-suffragists.**

2 **Visit the local-history section of your public library and find out if there was a suffragist or suffragette branch in your area. Were there any reports about it in the newspapers of the time?**

3 **The Museum of London, London Wall, EC2, has a large collection of suffragette material. The Fawcett Library at the London Guildhall University, Old Castle Street, Whitechapel, London E1, is Britain's main historical research library for women's studies. Also of interest are the Pankhurst Centre, Manchester, and the Glasgow People's Palace, which houses the Scottish Suffragette Fellowship collection.**

'The Shrieking Sister', a famous Punch *cartoon of 1906, showing the attitudes of the two sides in the suffrage movement. 'You help our cause?' says the woman on the left. 'Why, you're its worst enemy.' What does she mean? Whose side is the cartoonist on?*

Force Feeding

After a hunger strike of nearly four days (80 hours) I was fed by force without my heart being tested or my pulse felt . . . In spite of the first-hand accounts I had heard of this process, the reality surpassed all that I had anticipated – it was a living nightmare of pain, horror and revolting degradation. The sensation is of being strangled, suffocated by the thrust-down of the large rubber tube . . . There is also a feeling of complete helplessness, as of an animal in a trap, when the operators come into one's cell and set to work.

Do you think the government was right to order the forcible feeding of suffragettes? Was it a sensible move politically?

Letter from Lady Constance Lytton to The Times, *1 January 1910*

By 1910 it began to look as if the women's franchise might become a reality. Joint action by the WSPU and the NUWSS, which still had a far larger membership, persuaded the government to set up a committee to draw up a franchise bill. In return Mrs Pankhurst agreed to cease all militant activities.

A bill was actually presented to Parliament, but was withdrawn by the Prime Minister, Asquith. A suffragette protest at Westminster turned into a six-hour riot in which fifty women were seriously injured and two later died. Though the NUWSS agreed to work peacefully for a new franchise bill, the WSPU was enraged. A fresh campaign of violence was begun, in which window-smashing was official policy. In retaliation, police raided the WSPU offices and arrested Mr and Mrs Pethick-Lawrence. Emmeline Pankhurst was already in prison, but Christabel fled to France, leaving Annie Kenney to carry on her work in England.

In 1913, with nearly 100 suffragettes on hunger strike in prison, there was a public outcry against forcible feeding. In the House of Commons the Labour leader George Lansbury crossed the floor to shake his fist in Asquith's face, shouting, 'You will go down in history as the man who tortured innocent women!' In response to such criticism, the government devised the Prisoners (Temporary Discharge for Ill Health) Act, under which hunger strikers were released from prison to regain their strength and then rearrested and returned to their cells. It became known as the 'Cat and Mouse Act' because it was felt the government was playing with the suffragettes in the way a cat plays with a mouse. Mrs Pankhurst was imprisoned and released so many times under the Cat and Mouse Act that the London *Evening Standard* estimated that it would take her eighteen years to serve the three years' penal servitude to which she was sentenced in 1913.

Not long before the First World War broke out, a dramatic – and tragic – protest brought home to the general public the suffragettes' devotion to their cause. Emily Wilding Davison was a seasoned WSPU campaigner who had been to prison eight

Women were encouraged to volunteer for war work in factories by posters such as this. What effect did their ability to do such jobs have on their status after the war?

times and force-fed on forty-nine occasions. In June 1913 she went to Epsom racecourse and, as the Derby runners thundered past Tattenham Corner, she ducked under the barrier and ran across the track, shouting 'Votes for Women!' She grabbed at the reins of King George V's horse Anmer but was bowled over. The *Daily Mirror* reported: 'Anmer struck her with his chest, and she was knocked over screaming. Blood rushed from her nose and mouth.' The horse turned a somersault and the jockey went flying, though neither was seriously injured. Emily Davison, however, who was fifty-nine, died later of head injuries. The WSPU organized a spectacular funeral procession in London before her coffin was taken to Morpeth, Northumberland, where she was buried. The WSPU motto 'Deeds not words' was engraved on her tombstone.

On 4 August 1914, the day the First World War broke out, Millicent Fawcett sent a message to her supporters: 'Women, your country needs you . . . we have another duty now. Let us show ourselves worthy of citizenship, whether our claim to it be recognized or not.'

The NUWSS opened a Women's Service Bureau, which helped organize the drafting of women for war work. The WSPU, too, threw itself behind the war effort. 'War was the only course for our country to take', wrote Christabel Pankhurst later. 'As suffragettes we could not be pacifists at any price.' In response the government announced that all suffragette sentences would be remitted: 'His Majesty is confident that they can be trusted not to stain the cause they have at heart by any further crime or disorder.'

Sylvia Pankhurst, however, *was* a pacifist. She denounced the war in her paper *The Dreadnought*

and continued to work for peace, women's suffrage and justice for the poor. Although a wave of patriotic fervour was sweeping the country, there were other women peace campaigners who agreed with her. Many joined the Women's International League for Permanent Peace, which was formed in 1915. Another organization, the Women's Peace Crusade, staged huge anti-war demonstrations.

In many ways the war changed for ever long-entrenched attitudes to women both as citizens and as workers. It was realized that they were responsible people who could do all sorts of jobs – physically arduous, skilled and even dangerous – which hitherto had carried a 'men-only' label. Long before the war was over new talks were started on the female franchise. Even Mr Asquith, the old enemy, gave in, conceding that women 'cannot fight in the sense of going out with rifles and so forth but . . . they have aided in the most effective way in the prosecution of the war.'

A new Ministry of Munitions was set up in 1915 under David Lloyd George, who was later to become Prime Minister. It handled the recruitment of women munitions workers who, with more and more men being sent to fight overseas, were the only people available to produce the guns and ammunition needed at the front. Opposition from the trade unions, who feared that men's employment rights would be 'diluted' by the 'substitution' of women workers, meant that stringent agreements were made concerning women's wages – usually less than men's – and the type of work they could do. The men's jobs were safeguarded for

their return after the war.

Women were also recruited to work on the railways, as bus and tram drivers and conductors, and on the land in a specially formed Women's Land Army. Policewomen appeared on the streets for the first time. The recruitment of women as volunteers to all three of the armed services (something which would have astonished the Victorians) also began during the First World War. Three corps were formed, the Women's Royal Naval Service (WRNS), the Women's Army Auxiliary Corps (WAAC) and, almost at the end of the war, the Women's Royal Air Force Service. Members were employed in behind-the-lines support services, as cooks, drivers and clerical workers, but the units were disbanded after the war.

We have seen how during the nineteenth century women received professional training as nurses for the first time. The war naturally increased the demand for nurses, and this was met partly by two nursing associations, both founded a few years earlier: the First Aid Nursing Yeomanry, known by its initials as FANY, and the Voluntary Aid Detachments Scheme, established by the Red Cross and Order of St John. Hundreds of VAD nurses trained in first aid were sent to assist in the field hospitals, and although they were resented as ignorant amateurs by some qualified nurses, they were treated as heroines by the soldiers and the general public.

One British nurse, Edith Cavell, became leader of an underground escape organization when Germany invaded Belgium. She was arrested and shot by a German firing squad in 1915.

'Let us show ourselves worthy of citizenship'

Deeds not Words

The thinking behind the suffragettes' militant action was explained by Christabel Pankhurst:

When any section of the community possesses the vote, they can organise and use that vote in order to secure redress of their grievances, or measures of social reform. But when any section of the community is voteless, then the only way in which the bargaining power of the vote can be obtained is by action. When classes of men demanded the vote, they showed far less patience than women have shown. Their methods were far more violent. They broke not windows only, but heads.

Do you think the justification of militancy given by Christabel Pankhurst is reasonable? How would you have set about getting votes for women?

From an article written by Christabel Pankhurst for Votes for Women, *8 March 1912, but suppressed by the Home Office. (Home Office papers, Public Record Office, HO 144/1054/ 187986)*

War Work

By mid-1918 women were performing many different roles in military and civilian life. These included:

Women members/employees

WAAC	41,000
VAD	8,000
Munitions work	947,000
Railways	56,000
Trams and buses	19,000
Police	1,000
Agricultural work, including Women's Land Army	113,000

Figures compiled from various sources and rounded to the nearest 1,000

Study the table and draw a bar chart to illustrate the figures. Which occupation gave employment to the largest number of women? Why do you think this was?

Emily Davison and the King's horse lie on the Epsom racecourse after the suffragette's 1913 Derby Day demonstration. Can you imagine what comments the racegoers would have made? Do you think many supported her protest?

A VAD nurse checks the engine of her motor ambulance before going to meet a train carrying wounded soldiers from the front near Etaples in France in 1917. Though not as skilled as professional nurses, the VADs were popular with the soldiers, and earned the nicknames 'Red Cross nurses' and 'rose(s) of no-man's land'.

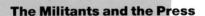

1 Read the extract from the *Evening Standard* again. What is the difference, in your view, between a thief and someone arrested for making a political protest? Should they be treated the same in prison?

2 The Imperial War Museum, Lambeth Road, London SE1, has a number of interesting displays showing the different kinds of work done by women during the First World War.

3 Read Chapter 8 of Vera Brittain's autobiography *Testament of Youth*, in which she describes her work as a VAD in a military hospital in France.

The Militants and the Press

The man who steals a silver-plated cake basket from a suburban villa may go to penal servitude for years . . . He is not released because he would rather not eat his dinner . . . Why . . . should exceptional favour be shown to female criminals on the grand scale? . . . The answer is simply that Ministers . . . are afraid that some utterly superfluous life should be ended, by a species of suicide, within the walls of a prison . . . It is simply fear that firmness . . . may lose votes and cause trouble with political cliques. In no other country in the world would it be possible for a handful of half-crazy women to set at defiance the whole machinery of law and justice.

Why did the newspaper describe suffragettes as 'half-crazy'? Do you think the *Standard* was right to say that the government brought in the Cat and Mouse Act because it was worried 'firmness' might lose votes?

From an article in the London Evening Standard, *13 March 1913*

Fifty years after her first speech in the campaign for women's suffrage, Millicent Fawcett at last achieved her goal. 'Votes for Women' became a reality on 7 February 1918, when a new Representation of the People Act gave the vote to all women over thirty – and all men over twenty-one. It was not until ten years later that this anomaly was put right and women were enfranchised on the same basis as men. Nevertheless, it was a time for celebration and when another act, passed the same year, enabled women to stand for Parliament, suffragists and suffragettes alike expected that at last women would start to take an equal part in the process of government.

Millicent Fawcett stood down as President of the NUWSS, which then adopted a new role and changed its name to the National Union of Societies for Equal Citizenship.

Christabel Pankhurst formed a new Women's Party and stood as its candidate in the 1918 general election. There were sixteen other female candidates, including the trade unionist Mary Macarthur, but only one, Constance Markiewicz, daughter of an Anglo-Irish landowner and wife of a Polish count, was elected. Ironically, she was a member of Sinn Fein, fighting for Irish independence, and refused to take her seat as MP for a Dublin constituency in the House of Commons. Christabel Pankhurst's defeat by 755 votes at Smethwick in the West Midlands saw the end of an attempt to create a political party specifically for women, an idea that had never had much support from either the moderates or militants in the suffrage movement.

Supporters of women's rights had to wait for a by-election in 1919 for the first female MP to enter Parliament. She was an unlikely candidate for the honour. The American-born wife of a British peer, Nancy Astor contested and won her husband's seat at Plymouth after he became Viscount Astor on the death of his father. She remained as Conservative MP for the constituency until 1945. The next two women MPs also replaced their husbands in safe seats, which was hardly the result the suffrage movement had hoped to achieve when women won the right to stand for Parliament.

By 1923, however, eight women had been elected on their own merits. There were now three female Labour MPs, including Margaret Bondfield, the first working-class woman to become an MP. A former shop assistant and trade-union activist, she also became the first woman cabinet minister and privy councillor in 1929 when Prime Minister Ramsey MacDonald made her Minister of Labour.

Eleanor Rathbone was elected as the first Independent (non-party) female MP in the same year. She fought ceaselessly for family allowances which, she maintained, would give married women dignity and remove the argument that men should have higher wages because they had families to support.

An important act of Parliament was passed at the end of 1919. The Sex Disqualification (Removal) Act gave women the right to enter professions such as the law and accountancy, from which they had previously been barred. It allowed the first female magistrates to be appointed and made women liable for jury service. Helena Normanton, later to become one of the first two female KCs (short for King's Counsel – senior barristers, now known as QCs or Queen's Counsel), was among the first women to be called to the Bar in 1922 and the first woman to fight a case in the High Court. Inevitably she and the other 'new lady barristers' were dubbed 'Portia' by the press after Shakespeare's heroine, who takes on the role of advocate in *The Merchant of Venice*.

Single women who, as teachers or secretaries, had a career rather than just a job were given the nickname 'bachelor girls' and admired for their independence. There were disadvantages, however. Female teachers and civil servants still did not have equal pay and a 'marriage bar' was operated, which meant that a woman had to give up her job if she got married. For many, however, marriage was not a possibility. As a result of the carnage in the trenches, there were about two million more women than men in Britain. Once again they were unkindly called 'surplus women'. Often it was hard for them to find a job, and for many in the working classes domestic service was still the only choice.

By necessity, the concept that 'a woman's place is in the home' had been challenged during the war when women were called on to hold down exacting jobs in the outside world. As a result of their wartime roles, women were more socially emancipated after 1918 than they had ever been. Fashions reflected this freer spirit and by the mid-twenties short skirts and short hair were the norm. In London's West End the 'Bright Young Things' or

the first female MP was an unlikely candidate for the honour

One of the first election posters aimed directly at women voters. Note the baby on the woman's arm and the mill chimney in the background. What message is the Labour Party putting across?

'flappers', as they were called, danced the Charleston to the new rhythms of jazz, smoked cigarettes, wore lipstick, spoke in slang, discussed 'free love' (sex outside marriage) and even swore – all things which would have been unthinkable before the war. They read novelists such as Virginia Woolf and D.H. Lawrence, who challenged the conventions of both fiction and society. Although Lawrence's sexually explicit novel *Lady Chatterley's Lover* was banned as an obscene publication in 1928, attitudes to sex *were* beginning to change.

Many young women, however, were still ignorant about sex and pregnancy, and most had only a very sketchy knowledge of methods of birth control. Abortion had been a criminal offence since 1861, so the only recourse for a woman with an unwanted pregnancy was a self-induced miscarriage or an illegal backstreet abortion, both extremely hazardous to health.

Although Marie Stopes took a degree in Botany and became a doctor of science, she knew nothing of sexual matters when she married for the first time. She longed for a baby and could not understand why she did not become pregnant. In fact her husband was impotent and the marriage was never consummated. Stopes later married again and had a son. In 1918 she published two pioneering books, *Married Love* and *Wise Parenthood*, which advocated contraception. In 1921 she opened Britain's first birth-control centre, the Mother's Clinic, in London. Even though it restricted advice to married

MOTHERS-VOTE LABOUR

Published by the Labour Party, Transport House (South Block) Smith Square, London S.W.1. and Printed by Vincent Brooks, Day & Son, LTD 48, Parker Street, Kingsway, W.C.2.

women, it was bitterly opposed, especially by the churches.

In the years following the First World War, many women had more freedom than ever before, but there was also a dark side to this post-war period. By the early twenties an economic slump had begun to cast its shadow over the hopes people had for a new and better life. In the 1930s, Britain, in common with America and other countries, was plunged into severe economic depression with unemployment reaching unprecedented levels. Workers staged anti-government hunger marches.

It was a woman, Ellen Wilkinson, the Labour MP for Jarrow in north-east England (one of the most distressed areas), who came to symbolize the heart of this protest. She marched at the head of the Jarrow Crusade in 1936 when 200 of the town's unemployed, thrown out of work by the closure of its shipyard, walked to London to present a petition signed by 11,000 people.

Among the First

When I accepted the Ministry of Labour, I did so knowing well that it touched much more than merely my own self – it was part of the great revolution in the position of women which had taken place in my lifetime and which I had done something to help forward. Some woman was bound to be first. That I should be was the accident of dates and events.

From A Life's Work *by Margaret Bondfield (1948)*

My tiny niche in history is that in that election [1929] I was a 'flapper voter' – one of the first batch of women entitled to vote at twenty-one on the same terms as men. I went to the polling station in a scarlet frock, a little disappointed that putting a cross on a bit of paper was so undramatic.

From Forgetting's No Excuse *by Mary Stott (1973)*

What important changes is Margaret Bondfield referring to when she talks of 'the great revolution in the position of women'? What is the voting age for women and men today?

Dr Stopes's Crusade

. . . the only right rule in marriage is that which gives the greatest sum total of health and happiness to the two concerned, for the benefit of the nation and the race . . .

Some, who would otherwise welcome the spread of knowledge on this important subject, fear an increase of promiscuous relations as a result. It appears, however, that the type of person who desires to lead an irregular life has long had access to sufficient information to satisfy such requirements, while the virtuous mother has been helpless in her ignorance of how to control her motherhood in the interest of her children.

Compare Marie Stopes's reasons for advocating birth control with those of Annie Besant (p. 10). Why do you think it took nearly fifty years from Besant's initial campaign for the first birth-control clinic to be opened? How had public opinion changed during this time?

From Wise Parenthood *by Marie Stopes (1918)*

▶ *Marie Stopes (seated) with her staff outside her family-planning clinic in Holloway Road, north London, in 1921. Why do you think the clinic treated only married women?*

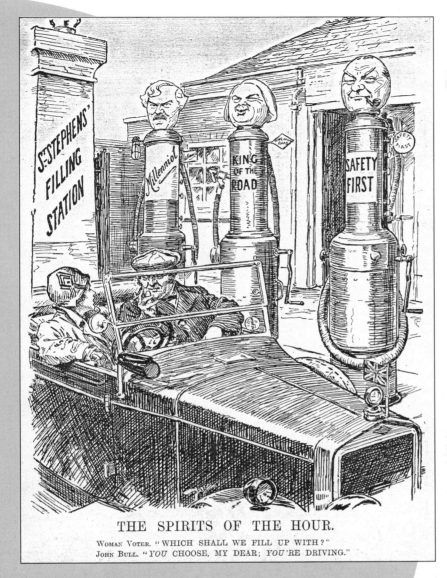

THE SPIRITS OF THE HOUR.

WOMAN VOTER. "WHICH SHALL WE FILL UP WITH?"
JOHN BULL. "YOU CHOOSE, MY DEAR; YOU'RE DRIVING."

The 1929 election was the first at which women voted on equal terms with men. The heads on the petrol pumps are those of the three party leaders, from left to right: Ramsay Macdonald (Labour), David Lloyd George (Liberal) and Stanley Baldwin (Conservative). What is the attitude of the cartoonist to women voters?

1 Assess the relative importance in gaining the vote of the suffragists' peaceful persuasion, the suffragettes' militant action, and the contribution of women to the war effort.

2 Do you know anyone who was a 'flapper voter' in 1929? Ask her what it felt like to be making history in this way.

3 Does your reference library or record office have any local newspapers from this period? How did they cover election day in 1929? What space did they give to the 'flapper vote'?

4 Look in your public library for jazz music from the 1920s by artists such as Louis Armstrong (Satchmo), Duke Ellington, Jelly Roll Morton and Blues singer Bessie Smith. Do you know how to dance the Charleston? What other dances were popular in the twenties?

5 Read Virginia Woolf's feminist essay *A Room of One's Own*. What does it tell you about feminist thought at the time?

Two Nations

The 1920s was a decade of paradoxes, of surface gaiety and hidden misery, of a generation dedicated to the pursuit of happiness in terms of sex freedom, and to good times in terms of cocktail parties, dancing night life, but all of it a gaudy superstructure imposed on the black, rotting foundation of the economic depression. London was one thing; industrial England another. It was two nations: two worlds.

What is the meaning of the word 'paradox'? How far do you think women had succeeded in achieving equality with men by this time?

From Young in the Twenties *by Ethel Mannin (1971), quoted in Graham Mitchell,* The Roaring Twenties *(1986)*

The problem of unemployment in Jarrow and other distressed areas had disappeared by 1939 not, sadly, through government action or economic recovery but because of rearmament and the outbreak of the Second World War in September of that year. Once again all available men were mobilized to help the war effort and by the end of the year more than 1½ million were in the armed forces. It was therefore the women who bore the brunt of nightly air-raids, the black-out, food rationing and 'making-do'.

In a massive effort organized by the government and supervised by the Women's Voluntary Service (WVS), 1½ million children were evacuated from the major cities, where intense bombing was expected, to the comparative safety of the country. It was a traumatic experience both for the children, despatched into the unknown with just a few possessions, a gas mask and a name tag pinned to their coats, and for the mothers who had to part with them. By the time the Blitz really started, in September 1940, the strain of separation had become so great that vast numbers of evacuees had returned home to face the bombing with their families.

Many women volunteered for war work in the early days of the war but in 1941 the government brought in conscription. All women aged between eighteen and forty (later fifty) could be directed into the services, into munitions factories, the ship-building or aircraft industries, or to work in transport, civil defence or the Women's Land Army. Those with children under the age of fourteen were exempt, but by 1943 there were 7½ million women in full-time employment.

Government propaganda made munitions work sound not only vitally important but exciting as well. In reality most women workers found it boring and monotonous. Many had to work a sixty-hour week in noisy, dirty conditions. Under restrictions imposed by the black-out, there was often little ventilation or light. 'Working in a factory is not fun', one twenty-year-old told the Mass Observation social-survey unit. 'Boredom is our worst enemy.'

Two-years before the end of the war, four out of five married

women were doing war work and about a third of these had children at home. However, the Labour Research Department reported that thousands of women could still not take jobs because of 'low wages, insufficient day nurseries, long working hours and consequent shopping difficulties'. Nursery provision was obviously essential. Women, eager to help the war effort, staged protest marches demanding 'Nurseries for Kids, War Work for Mother'. By 1944, though a large number of children were still cared for by relatives or friends while their mothers were 'doing their bit', there were more than 1,000 local-authority nurseries in operation.

Shopping had been a particular problem for working mothers ever since food rationing was introduced in January 1940. A family's ration books could only be registered at one grocer's and at one butcher's, and these shops closed early, especially in winter,

Many had to work a sixty-hour week in noisy, dirty conditions

to save power. The arrival of unrationed goods, such as fruit, meant long queues – and those at the end got nothing!

The working woman's dual role was given official recognition in 1942 when the Ministry of Labour called on managements to 'recognise frankly that many workers, especially women, cannot be expected to work five and a half days a week, for long hours, week in week out . . . if they have homes and young children to look after'. In many factories hours were staggered, and in some cases women were allowed time off for shopping.

The question of wages was less easily resolved. Though some women were given pay equal to that of men doing the same work, women's wages were usually considerably lower. As in the First World War male workers and trade unions were concerned that women should not hold on to 'men's jobs' once the war ended.

In the engineering industry agreement was reached with the unions that women would be taken on as temporary war workers and paid the man's rate for the job if they were doing it without 'special assistance, guidance or supervision'.

Qu 3

Women munitions workers making shells. What other types of war work did women do between 1939 and 1945?

Employers got round this in various ways. A female shop steward complained in 1941, for instance, that 'a man is employed to do lifting, maybe only small trays, but this prevents women from earning a man's wages'.

The Women's Land Army was re-formed just before the war started. More than 200,000 women were recruited between 1939 and 1950, when the WLA was disbanded, responding with alacrity to posters that urged them: 'For a healthy, happy job – join the Women's Land Army'.

Women in the armed forces were not sent out to fight, yet the work they did as non-combatants was difficult and dangerous. During the war, half a million women put on uniform and went into what were known as the auxiliary services: the Women's Royal Naval Service (WRNS), the Auxiliary Territorial Service (ATS) and the Women's Auxiliary Air Force (WAAF).

Servicewomen worked on anti-aircraft 'ack-ack' batteries, as searchlight crews, wireless operators, bomb-loaders and motor-cycle despatch riders. Some flew planes as members of the Air Transport Auxiliary, which delivered aircraft from the factories to their squadrons.

One of the ATA members was Amy Johnson, the pioneer aviator who in 1930 became the first woman to fly solo to Australia. An experienced – and world-famous – pilot, she was disappointed that, as a female, this was the only kind of flying she was allowed to do in wartime. In 1941 Johnson's plane crashed in bad weather into the Thames estuary, making her one of fourteen women ferry pilots killed during the war. Altogether more than 600 members of the women's forces were killed on active service and 700 wounded.

Photo Copy.

Servicewomen

When several of us were selected to train as radar operators or operators fire control (OFCs) we went off for six gruelling weeks of training at a large camp near Oswestry. There we learnt about electricity, radar, radio, maintenance of equipment. It was all very secret then . . . After that we went to a firing camp at Anglesey and joined the remainder of what was to be our AA battery of the future: gunners, predictor operators, height-finders, spotters, telephonists, cooks, orderlies and, of course, our officers. I found the noise of the guns at such close range ear-splitting at first.

Ruth Negus, ATS, who worked on an anti-aircraft (AA) battery, quoted in Eric Taylor, Women Who Went to War *(1988)*

What roles were women in the ATS, WRNS and WAAF *not* allowed to take on during the war?

This wartime advertisement stresses the woman's dual role. What other factors, apart from an easier wash-day, helped women to cope?

The Kitchen Front

The most famous wartime recipe was Woolton pie, named after Lord Woolton, the Minister of Food:

5 to 6 persons. Ingredients can be varied according to vegetables in season. Take 1 lb each of diced potatoes, cauliflower, swedes and carrots, three or four spring onions, if possible, one teaspoonful of vegetable extract and one tablespoonful of oatmeal. Cook all together for 10 minutes, with just enough water to cover. Stir occasionally to prevent the mixture from sticking. Allow to cool. Put in a pie dish, sprinkle with chopped parsley and cover with a crust of potatoes or wholemeal pastry. Bake in a moderate oven until the pastry is nicely browned.

From the Ministry of Food 'Kitchen Front' booklet (1942)

Sugar and meat were in short supply during the war. Do you think a Woolton pie would be more healthy than the kind of food we eat today?

The Dual Role

. . . for me, as a man, it is a matter of admiration and respect that women with household responsibilities should not merely be working in industry but should become the elected spokesmen and trusted representatives of their fellow workers. We men, of the AEU, know what an active member's life and shop steward's duties mean; the endless, sometimes tiresome detailed work, the patience, the tact, the resoluteness, all voluntarily expended; but we do not also have to think of the housework, the washing and shopping, the kids' breakfast and the old man's tea.

How do women cope with the dual role today? Do labour-saving devices and convenience food make a difference? Do husbands give more support to working wives than in the past?

From a speech at the first AEU Women's Conference, given by the President, Jack Tanner, and quoted in Sarah Boston, Women Workers and the Trade Unions *(1987)*

1 Make a Woolton pie, or try some of the wartime recipes from *We'll Eat Again* by Marguerite Patten or *Bombers and Mash* by Raynes Minns (see p. 47).

2 Do you know anyone who was *either* an evacuee *or* a housewife during the Second World War? Ask them about their experiences.

3 The Imperial War Museum, London, and the Eden Camp Museum, Malton, North Yorkshire, have a number of exhibits and displays on women's work and experiences during the years 1939–45.

In the Factory

In the factory we were allocated to different sections. The girls that were really A1 were put into the part that made the most dangerous shells and bullets. I was sent to make bullets, small bombs and shells. We used TNT, gelignite and neonite. The work was dangerous, sometimes people got fingers blown off or it could be more serious. You just got used to it. If you worked with TNT, you'd get a nice rash and also your face and hair would go yellow. The work was always boring, but there was always someone near to you to chat to.

How could work in a munitions factory be both dangerous and boring at the same time? Do you think having someone to chat to would make up for the monotony?

Oral interview with Mrs Groves, a former munitions worker, quoted in Caroline Lang, Keep Smiling Through *(1989)*

SEE HOW THEY GROW!

JUNE 39 DEC 39 DEC 1940 DECEMBER 1941 DECEMBER 1942

WAAF WOMAN-POWER

▶ *A recruiting poster of 1942, showing the new WAAF uniform. Compare this with the clothes worn by the VAD on pp. 26–7. How do they differ? Which would be best for wartime work?*

Photo copy.

The immediate post-war years were known as 'the years of austerity' Food, clothing and fuel were still in short supply; rationing dragged on into the 1950s. As had happened after the First World War, many women workers gave up their jobs. This time, however, there were no 'surplus women' because far more 'boys' came 'marching home' than had been the case in 1918. The number of early marriages rose and there was a brief baby boom.

Married women retreated to a low-profile existence as housewives and mothers. Even graduate wives astonished earlier feminists by opting for domesticity rather than the workplace. Though there was a shortage of labour, the need for mothers to stay at home and look after their children was continually stressed. The wartime nurseries closed down.

A paper produced for the World Health Organization on *Maternal Deprivation and Mental Health* by Dr John Bowlby inspired the new thinking on childcare. Bowlby had been writing about children in institutions, but mothers at home seized on a paperback published in 1953 which expounded his theories in a more readable fashion. *Child Care and the Growth of Love* became the 'Mothers' Bible' of the fifties. Its ideas concerning 'the absolute need of infants and toddlers for the continuous care of their mothers' were reinforced by an American childcare manual published in England in 1955. Dr Benjamin Spock's *The Common Sense Book of Baby and Child Care* was so popular that its worldwide sale reached 20 million copies. Dr Bowlby later maintained that he had been misinterpreted, and had never meant to suggest that mothers stay with their children twenty-four hours a day.

In the general election of 1945 a Labour government was returned. It brought in legislation to set up a Welfare State, which had been proposed in the Beveridge Report of 1942. These new measures were hailed as a charter for social security 'from the cradle to the grave' and included protection against sickness and unemployment, and old-age pensions payable to women as well as men. Family allowances were introduced in 1946, to be paid directly to the mother rather than the father: something that the MP Eleanor Rathbone had fought for since 1917.

The king-pin of the new Welfare State was the National Health Service, which came into being in 1948, with free medical and

Cilla Black, one of the women pop stars of the 1960s, hosting a television programme. What is she famous for today? Can you name any other women singers of the period?

hospital treatment for all. For women especially, this was an immense advance. Before the war, men paying National-Insurance contributions had been entitled to free medical treatment but their wives and families had not.

Comprehensive maternity services were now set up and home births – once the norm – began to decline as midwives moved away from the community into hospital practice. A Natural

Childbirth Trust was formed in 1956 to improve the pregnant woman's knowledge of childbirth and help her deal with pain through relaxation rather than drugs.

Gradually it became acceptable for the father to attend the baby's birth, and men began to take a greater share in looking after the children. But despite their husbands' help, many young women led an isolated existence. Once, an extended family of parents, sisters, aunts and grandparents living close by had made child-rearing a shared experience. Now, in the expanding suburbs and new towns, they often felt lonely and cut off.

An article published in *The Guardian* by Betty Jerman in 1960 sparked off a correspondence which led to the formation of a National Housewives' Register of 'lively-minded women' who could contact each other for activities that ranged from baby-minding to political debates. The membership grew to 25,000.

Birth control was at last respectable for married women, and the Family Planning Association (founded in 1931 as the National Birth Control Association) vastly increased the number of its clinics in the 1950s. In 1958 the Church of England gave contraception its blessing.

Contraceptive advice remained difficult for unmarried women to obtain until 1964 when Helen Brook started the Brook Advisory Centres. Until the contraceptive pill was introduced, however, birth-control methods were not dependable. The Pill – available to married and unmarried alike from 1967 – brought sexual freedom and, above all, choice to the women who used it. From 1974 it was provided free on the NHS.

Even in the 'permissive society' of the 1960s many young women were still ignorant or careless of contraceptive methods. During this decade the illegitimacy rate rose from 5.8% to 8.2% of all live births. Under the rigid moral code of an earlier age, unmarried mothers had been seen as 'fallen women'; now attitudes began to mellow. More divorces added to the numbers of one-parent families.

Since 1923 grounds for divorce had been the same for women as for men. In 1969 a new law abolished the need to prove a 'matrimonial offence' such as adultery and made it possible for couples to divorce if their marriage had irretrievably broken down.

An Abortion Law Reform Association had been founded in 1936 to try to bring to an end the illegal back-street abortions which endangered women's lives. Its leaders, who included Dora Russell, a feminist writer and peace campaigner, believed that the law should enshrine a woman's right to control her own body. However, it was not until the more liberal sixties that the reformers got their way. In 1967 an Abortion Act was passed making it possible for a woman to have an abortion on health grounds if two doctors agreed it was necessary. The operation could take place on the NHS or in a private clinic. The Act caused much controversy and was opposed especially by the Catholic Church. Supporters of the anti-abortion movement tried to get it repealed or altered on moral and religious grounds, and this campaign has continued to the present day.

The late 1950s saw the growth of a new and affluent society in which household appliances like refrigerators and washing machines were available to many, television sets (a rarity before the war) were widely owned, and foreign food and foreign holidays were becoming fashionable. Despite – or perhaps because of – this, married women began to jib at an everyday existence wholly devoted to housework and childcare.

For single women in an economy characterized by full employment, there had never been any going back to the restrictive pre-war days. Wartime work had brought independence. They had more freedom in their personal lives too, especially during the so-called 'Swinging Sixties' – a time of liberation, relaxed morals and a youth culture that revelled in new music like that of The Beatles, new fashions in dress and new attitudes to sexual relationships. In 1961 Penguin Books decided to test the Obscene Publications Act (1959) by publishing an uncut edition of D.H. Lawrence's *Lady Chatterley's Lover*, banned since 1928. A trial resulted in which many well-known writers were called to give evidence. They stated that, in their opinion, as the book was a work of literature, the explicit sex scenes were a necessary part of its artistic whole. The jury decided that the book was not an obscene publication, and this verdict has been described by some as marking the start of the 'permissive society' of the 1960s.

Against this background there sprang up a new feminist movement, which was to have a profound influence on women's lives.

new fashions in dress and new attitudes to sexual relationships

Childcare and Dr Spock

The important thing for a mother to realize is that the younger the child the more necessary it is for him to have a steady, loving person taking care of him. In most cases, the mother is the best one to give him this feeling of 'belonging', safely and surely . . . If a mother realizes clearly how vital this kind of care is to a small child, it may make it easier for her to decide that the extra money she might earn, or the satisfaction she might receive from an outside job, is not so important after all.

From The Common Sense Book of Baby and Child Care *by Dr Benjamin Spock (1946)*

The anthropologist Margaret Mead, however, described this theory as follows:

. . . a new and subtle form of anti-feminism in which men – under the guise of exalting the importance of maternity – are tying women more tightly to their children than has been thought necessary since the invention of bottle-feeding and baby-carriages.

From an article by Margaret Mead, published in the American Journal of Orthopsychiatry, *July 1954. Quoted in Ruth Adam,* A Woman's Place *(1975)*

Why do you think Dr Spock's book had such a great influence? If you were a young mother would you want to stay at home to look after your baby or go out to work?

Lady Chatterley on Trial

You may think that one of the ways in which you can test this book, and test it from the most liberal outlook, is to ask yourselves the question, when you have read it through, would you approve of your young sons, young daughters – because girls can read as well as boys – reading this book? Is it a book that you would have lying around in your house? Is it a book that you would even wish your wife or your servants to read?

From the opening address for the prosecution by Mr M. Griffith-Jones, quoted in C.H. Rolph (ed.), The Trial of Lady Chatterley *(1961)*

Compare this source with the remarks made by the prosecuting counsel in the Knowlton pamphlet case (see p. 10). How far did the verdict in the *Lady Chatterley* trial mean that such attitudes were changing?

▲

This cartoon is based on a deliberate misunderstanding. What point is cartoonist Mel Calman making? Why is the woman so much bigger than the man?

Photo Copy

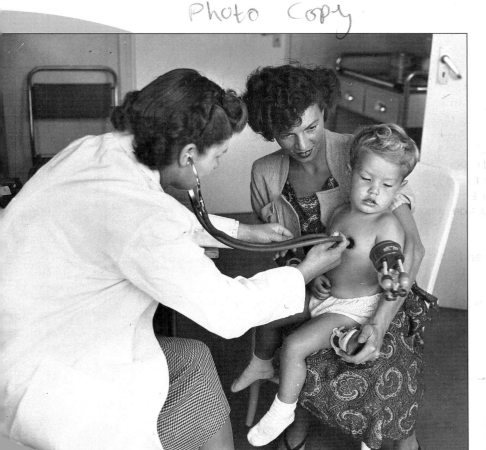

A doctor tests a child at the Woodberry Down Health Centre in 1952. The centre was the first of its kind to be built under the National Health Service Act. What benefits did mothers and children gain from the NHS in its early years?

1 Why do you think women reverted to domesticity after the war? Why were nursery facilities provided during the war but not afterwards?

2 Interview friends or relatives who grew up and started work in the 1950s or 1960s. Ask them about such things as educational opportunities, leisure pursuits, career choices, parental authority and sexual relationships. How do their experiences compare with yours?

3 Find out about the pop music of the 1960s. (You can borrow cassettes and CDs from your local library.) Who were the women pop stars in the sixties? Suggest ways in which the music differs from that of today.

4 The following first novels, all written from the female point of view, give an insight into the lives of young people in the 1950s and 1960s: *The L-Shaped Room* (1959) by Lynne Reid Banks, *A Summer Bird-Cage* (1963) by Margaret Drabble, *Up the Junction* (1963) by Nell Dunn and *Georgy Girl* (1965) by Margaret Forster.

Dancing Days

A woman who was a teenager in the mid-1950s recalled her youth thirty years later on a television programme:

I used to go to the Plaza every dinner-time. It cost us sixpence for two hours. The thousands that used to go there! They had it on from twelve till two, and I only had an hour for my dinner. I used to sneak the two hours and creep into work so that nobody would see me. But I wasn't on my own – everybody else was doing the same, and of course at that time you could walk in a job and get sacked, then go and get another job in the afternoon. It was that easy to go and get jobs.

Do you think people have a tendency to remember only the good things about the past? What disadvantages might teenage girls have faced in the 1950s?

From You'll Never Be Sixteen Again *by Peter Everett, BBC Publications (1985)*

The women's liberation movement started in America with the publication in 1963 of a book called *The Feminine Mystique*. The author, Betty Friedan, shocked the American public with her crusade to 'raise the consciousness of women'. The 'women's libbers', as they became known, campaigned against all the fetters that still held women back, including sexual harassment and male prejudice, sex-discrimination in schools and in the workplace, inferior rates of pay and lack of job opportunities. They backed the pro-abortion movement and called for new curbs on domestic violence.

By the late sixties the movement had spread to Britain and women's groups were set up in numerous towns. A national conference was held in 1970. In *The Female Eunuch*, an influential book published that year, Germaine Greer argued that women's roles as wives and mothers prevented them from reaching their full potential.

The 'marriage bar' for teachers and employees in the civil service and local government had been abolished during the war. In 1955 equal pay was agreed for these professions, and in 1963 a TUC Charter for Women demanded equal pay for all. Five years later a turning point for manual workers was reached when a strike of women sewing-machinists brought the Ford motor factory in Dagenham, near London, to a standstill. The women claimed that their work was as skilled as that done by men who earned more. They were persuaded to accept 92% of the male rate after mediation by the Employment Minister, Barbara Castle.

Mrs Castle, a Labour MP and fiery campaigner for women's rights, promised to start talks on equal pay. In 1970 these bore fruit with the first of a number of Acts of Parliament which were to change the status of women in Britain.

The Equal Pay Act laid down that by 1975 men and women doing the same jobs should receive the same pay. It still left a lot of women earning much less, however, because where the jobs they did differed even slightly from those done by men, they were usually paid less. This was really the point the Dagenham strikers had been arguing but it was not until 1984 that an Equal Value Amendment was added to the Equal Pay Act to ensure that equal pay should be given for similar work if it was judged to be of equal value.

In 1975 an Employment Protection Act made it illegal to dismiss a woman from her job because she was pregnant. With certain restrictions it provided for maternity leave, maternity pay, and the right of a woman to return to her job after the birth of her baby. In the same year the Sex Discrimination Act was passed, banning any discrimination against a person because of their sex, in employment, education, and advertising, and in the provision of homes, goods and services. An Equal Opportunities Commission was set up to see that the Act was observed. Inequality, however, still persisted, and the EOC had to investigate numerous cases of discrimination in workplaces and schools.

The winning of equal opportunities did not result in the sudden emergence of women in top jobs. Feminists blamed sexual stereotyping at home and in schools and talked of a 'glass ceiling' that prevented women reaching top management positions. In politics, too, women found it difficult to compete on an equal basis with men. The House of Commons, with its late-night debates and atmosphere of a men's club, did not suit women with family commitments. Many constituency parties were reluctant to adopt women parliamentary candidates so, in

A financial executive at work. Although banking is still a male-dominated profession, an increasing number of women are reaching senior positions. What problems might they encounter?

1980, an all-party organization, The 300 Group, was formed to campaign for more women in Parliament. Its aim was a minimum of 300.

Though a scarce breed, women MPs have usually been of high calibre and many have been outstanding. Perhaps it is not surprising, therefore, that Britain should have been one of the first countries in the world to have a woman Prime Minister. What would have surprised the early women's rights campaigners was the woman who stepped into this role: Margaret Thatcher was in no way a feminist but a die-hard Conservative. She was elected to Parliament as MP for Finchley in 1959, was appointed Education Minister in 1970 and became party leader five years later. When the Conservatives won the 1979 general election she entered No. 10 Downing Street. She was to be Prime Minister for eleven years.

The appointment of a woman Prime Minister was only one of many landmarks in a century that had seen great achievements in the fight by women for equal rights and opportunities. Throughout the years of Mrs Thatcher's premiership, however, women still lagged behind men in terms of pay and career prospects. The old obstacle of the dual role had never been resolved and an economic recession in the early 1990s meant that women could not, as had been hoped, demand childcare provision and career breaks. Many had to settle for part-time employment and by the end of 1993 eight out of ten part-timers – mostly low-waged – were women.

Though the number of women in top jobs slowly increased in the nineties, there were still only a small number in Parliament and only two in John Major's Cabinet. A record forty-seven women MPs were elected in 1987, including Dianne Abbott, the first black woman MP, but this figure was only 6% of the total. In 1992 the number increased to fifty-nine out of a total of 650.

During the 1980s, campaigners such as Dora Russell were still active in peace movements, notably the Campaign for Nuclear Disarmament (founded in 1958). In 1981 a women's peace camp was set up outside the US air base at Greenham Common, Berkshire, to protest against the siting there of nuclear Cruise missiles. It remained until the missiles were removed in 1993.

a 'glass ceiling' prevented women reaching top management positions

By contrast, changes in the women's services opened up some fighting roles to women. From 1990 members of the WRNS could serve in warships, and in 1993, when their service was fully integrated with the Royal Navy, they were allowed to take on full combat duties at sea. Though the WRAC was integrated with the army in the same year, service-women were still barred from front-line fighting duties. RAF women, however, became eligible to train as pilots of combat aircraft in 1991. In that year astronaut Helen Sharman was chosen for the Anglo-Soviet Juno space mission and became the first British person to go into space.

A step towards equality of the sexes in religious matters was taken by the Church of England in 1993 when its General Synod (governing body) voted in favour of the ordination of women priests. Though non-conformist churches already had women ministers, there was much opposition to this move among some sections of the Church of England.

What the future brings for women in society now depends to a large extent on the attitudes and actions of young people still at school. These citizens of the twenty-first century may yet be needed to carry on the great revolution in women's lives, about which Margaret Bondfield wrote, and to finish the job started so long ago by pioneers like Barbara Bodichon, Annie Besant and Emmeline Pankhurst.

Women in Politics

I certainly find I am pushed to the limit of impossibility. You get your sleep down to 5½ hours a night. The basic question is how you fit everything in; it all comes back to you. After I get home with my red box I have to make the dinner and by the time I start on my box it's half past eleven at night. I manage it because I am physically terribly strong, and I live nearby and I dash to and fro. And I used to have a good daily help. But there's very little time for private or domestic life.

Shirley Williams (Labour cabinet minister) quoted in Melanie Phillips, The Divided House *(1980)*

I haven't just come to this out of the blue. I've been in politics for thirty years now. In British politics you don't just go from the bottom to the top – you climb your way up the ladder. I just hope that people will take me as I am for what I can do, not as a man or woman but as a personality who has an absolute passion for getting things right for Britain! I just can't bear Britain in decline . . . I just hope they'll . . . say, 'Does it really matter whether it's a man or a woman, isn't it just better to get things right?'

Margaret Thatcher in a BBC TV Panorama *interview with Michael Cockerell, 1979. Quoted in Patricia Murray,* Margaret Thatcher *(1980)*

Do you think a male MP would have found himself beset by the same problems as Shirley Williams? Why did Margaret Thatcher say she wanted to be regarded as a personality rather than a man or woman? Do you think a man would have said the same thing on becoming Prime Minister?

Some of the first women priests of the Church of England, pictured after their ordination in Bristol Cathedral on 12 March 1994.

◀

Unfair Dismissal

The first case of sexual harassment to be brought to a tribunal with the backing of the EOC was that of Ellie Walsh, a recruitment officer who was sacked when she poured lager over her firm's accountant. She won the case and was awarded damages.

She was at an office party in a local nightclub when the incident happened . . . an accountant working for the firm kept interrupting the conversation she was having with some women employees. He tried lifting her up over the bar and he put his hands round her neck. Ellie claimed that he kept prodding and touching her. He then grabbed hold of her arm and she slapped him. He tried pushing a glass of lager into her hands. 'Then I took the glass off him and poured it over him', said Ellie . . . He came back later and said, 'As from an hour ago you are sacked!'
    Her dismissal was later confirmed by the managing director . . . Her solicitor . . . told the tribunal: 'What happened that night was sexual harassment. It could not have happened but for the fact that she was a woman.'

Why do you think the accountant acted as he did? What was he trying to prove?

From a report in Equality Now!, *the magazine of the EOC, autumn 1983*

◀

Women bus conductors stage a protest demonstration in December 1968. What is the main demand being made by these women? How did the position change after 1975?

1 Compare the Women's Movement since the 1960s with earlier campaigns for women's rights. What are the main differences?

2 Are you aware of any sex stereotyping or sex discrimination in your school? Is there much difference between the subjects girls and boys wish to study at GCSE and A Level? If so, why do you think this is?

3 Is the MP for the constituency you live in a man or a woman? Find out how many women MPs there are today. Your reference library should have the information.

4 Contact organizations such as the Institute of Bankers, the Institute of Civil Engineers and the Law Society (for solicitors) and find out whether the percentages of women working in these professions have changed since 1976. Another useful organization is:
Women in Management
64 Marryat Road
London SW19 5BN

5 Draw a cartoon reflecting attitudes to women in Britain today.

1850 North London Collegiate School opened by Frances Buss.

1854–5 Crimean War. Florence Nightingale nursing at Scutari.

1857 Matrimonial Causes Act gives women some property rights.

English Woman's Journal founded.

1859 Elizabeth Blackwell becomes the first woman to be entered on the Medical Register.

1866 First Women's Suffrage Committee formed by Barbara Bodichon.

1869 Women rate-payers given vote in local elections.

1870 Education Act – women allowed to serve on school boards.

Married Woman's Property Act – wives allowed to keep their earnings.

1873 Girton College (formed 1869) established at Cambridge.

1877 Custody of Infants Act – gives custody of children up to the age of sixteen to the mother.

1878 Women admitted to the University of London.

1882 Second Married Woman's Property Act – married women given same rights over property as single women.

1886 Repeal of the Contagious Diseases (CD) Acts of 1864, 1866 and 1869.

1888 Match girls' strike.

1897 National Union of Women's Suffrage Societies formed with Millicent Fawcett as President.

1903 Women's Social and Political Union formed by Emmeline Pankhurst and her daughters Christabel and Sylvia.

1906 National Federation of Women Workers founded by Mary Macarthur.

1907 Women allowed to sit on county and borough councils.

1914–18 First World War. Women active in war work.

1918 Representation of the People Act gives votes to women over thirty.

Parliament (Qualification of Women) Act enables women over twenty-one to stand for Parliament.

1919 Nancy Astor becomes the first woman MP.

Sex Disqualification (Removal) Act allows women to enter the law and other professions.

1921 Marie Stopes opens the first birth-control clinic.

1928 Equal Franchise Act gives votes to all women over twenty-one on the same basis as men.

1929 Margaret Bondfield becomes first woman cabinet minister.

1936 Ellen Wilkinson heads Jarrow hunger march.

1939–45 Second World War. Women conscripted for war work.

1945 Family Allowance Act gives weekly payments to mothers.

1948 National Health Service launched. Women students admitted to all medical schools.

1955 Equal pay introduced for teachers, civil servants and local-government officers.

1963 Publication of Betty Friedan's *The Feminine Mystique*. Start of the women's lib movement.

1967 Abortion Act legalizes abortion.

1969 Divorce Reform Act – divorcing couples no longer have to prove a 'matrimonial offence'.

1970 Equal Pay Act.

1975 Sex Discrimination Act.

Employment Protection Act – provides for maternity leave.

Equal Opportunities Commission set up.

1979 Margaret Thatcher becomes first woman Prime Minister.

1980 300 Group formed to fight for more women MPs.

1981 Greenham Common women's peace camp set up to protest against Cruise missiles.

1984 Equal Value Amendment to Equal Pay Act passed – equal pay given for different jobs of equal value.

1987 First black woman MP elected to the House of Commons with forty-six other female MPs.

1990 WRNS eligible to serve on warships.

1991 RAF servicewomen allowed to train as combat pilots.

1993 WRNS and WRAC integrated with men's services.

General Synod of the Church of England vote for the ordination of women priests.

1994 WRAF integrated with RAF.

First women priests ordained in the Church of England.

Elizabeth Garrett ANDERSON (1836–1917). Medical pioneer. As a woman, she was barred from medical school in 1860 but went on to open a women's dispensary in London (named the Elizabeth Garrett Anderson Hospital after her death). In 1870 she took a medical degree in Paris and in 1871 married James Anderson. She lectured at the London School of Medicine for Women founded by Sophia Jex-Blake and was the first woman member of the British Medical Association. In 1908 she became Britain's first woman mayor when she was elected to the office in her home town of Aldeburgh, Suffolk.

Nancy, Lady ASTOR, born Langhorne (1879–1964). Politician. Born in Virginia, USA, she married Waldorf Astor, son of the millionaire Viscount Astor, in 1906. Waldorf later became Conservative MP for Plymouth. When he inherited his father's title in 1919, she was elected in his place at a by-election and was the first woman to sit in the House of Commons. She remained an MP until 1945, speaking mainly on issues concerning women and the family. She often crossed swords with Winston Churchill.

Annie BESANT, born Wood (1847–1933). Social reformer. She married the Rev. Frank Besant in 1867 and was legally separated from him in 1873. A 'free-thinker', she was made vice-president of the National Secular Society in 1874 and in the following year was tried with Charles Bradlaugh MP for publishing a birth-control pamphlet. She founded a radical paper, *The Link*, in 1885 with journalist W.T. Stead, and joined the socialist Fabian Society. She led the match girls' strike in 1888 but in the following year was converted to the religious faith of Theosophy and went to live in India, where she championed the cause of self-government.

Barbara BODICHON, born Leigh-Smith (1827–91). Feminist. She attended Bedford College for Women and ran a school in London for ten years. She campaigned for the rights of married women and was one of the founders of the *English Woman's Journal*. In her book *Women's Work* (1857) she argued for paid work for

women. In 1867 she became secretary of the Women's Suffrage Committee, which she helped to found, and she was one of **Emily Davies**'s staunchest allies in the battle for university education for females.

Margaret BONDFIELD (1873–1953). Trade unionist and politician. Born in Chard, Somerset, the tenth child of a lace-maker, she became a shop assistant at fifteen. In 1894 she joined the National Union of Shop Assistants and was its full-time assistant secretary from 1898–1908. She took an active part in Labour politics and, though a pacifist, sat on a government advisory committee on women's wartime employment during the First World War. In 1923 she became the first woman to chair the TUC and in the same year was elected to Parliament as a Labour MP. Appointed Minister of Labour in 1929, she was the first woman cabinet minister. She lost her seat in the 1931 election and returned to trade-union work.

Barbara CASTLE, born Betts (1910–). Politician. Born in Bradford she went to the local girls' grammar school and won a scholarship to Oxford. She worked in the Ministry of Food during the war and in 1944 married Ted Castle, a journalist. She was elected Labour MP for Blackburn in 1945 and remained in the House of Commons until 1979 when she became a Member of the European Parliament. In the Labour governments of the 1960s and 1970s she held several ministerial posts, including Secretary of State for Social Services. Since 1990 she has sat in the House of Lords as Baroness Castle of Blackburn.

Emily DAVIES (1830–1921). Feminist and educational pioneer. Brought up in Gateshead, where her father was a Church of England rector, she met **Barbara Bodichon** in 1859 and started a North-East branch of the Society for Promoting the Employment of Women. In 1861 she moved to London and became joint-editor of the *Englishwoman's Journal*. In 1867 she formed a committee to work for women's university education and in 1869 founded Benslow House at Hitchin, which was later reopened in Cambridge as

Girton College. She was the first Mistress (Principal) of Girton until 1875, when she returned to London to work for the suffrage campaign.

Millicent FAWCETT, born Garrett (1847–1929). Suffragist. The younger sister of **Elizabeth Garrett Anderson**, she married Henry Fawcett, a Cambridge professor and radical MP. In 1867 she became a member of the Women's Suffrage Committee. She also campaigned for the Married Woman's Property Act with Barbara Bodichon. Elected first President of the National Union of Women's Suffrage Societies in 1887, she worked for the women's franchise until 1914, when she supported the war effort. In 1916, however, she renewed pressure for the vote, which was achieved in 1918. She was made a Dame of the British Empire in 1925.

Germaine GREER (1939–). Writer and lecturer. Born in Australia, she took degrees at Melbourne and Sydney universities before moving to England, where she gained a PhD at Cambridge. She taught English literature at Warwick University and also in America, where she founded the Tulsa Centre for the Study of Women's Literature in 1979. She later returned to England and became a lecturer at Newnham College, Cambridge. As well as her feminist work *The Female Eunuch* (1970), she has published several books on women's literature, including *The Uncollected Verse of Aphra Behn* (1989). In 1991 she published *The Change: Women, Ageing and the Menopause*.

Florence NIGHTINGALE (1820–1910). Nursing pioneer. Named after the Italian city where she was born, she was brought up to a life of leisure but was determined to become a nurse. During the Crimean War she led a party of nurses out to work in the military hospital at Scutari. Afterwards, money was raised by public subscription to enable her to found the Nightingale School of Nursing at St Thomas's Hospital, London. She also organized the reform of the Royal Army Medical Corps and, though an invalid for many years, initiated a government inquiry into the health of the army in India. In 1907 she was the first woman to be awarded the Order of Merit.

Emmeline PANKHURST, born Goulden (1858–1928). Suffragette. The eldest of ten children of a Manchester calico printer, she was brought up in a radical family and attended suffrage meetings with her mother. In 1879 she married Dr Richard Pankhurst, a barrister, and worked with him for the North of England Society for Women's Suffrage. He died in 1898 and in 1903 she and two of their daughters, Christabel and Sylvia, founded the militant Women's Social and Political Union, whose members became known as suffragettes. During her 'Votes for Women' campaign she was gaoled and force-fed many times, often appearing at suffragette meetings on a stretcher.

Marie STOPES, born Carmichael (1880–1958). Birth-control pioneer. Born in Edinburgh, she trained as a botanist and gained a doctorate at Munich in 1904. Her marriage to a Canadian botanist was annulled in 1916 and her unhappy marital experiences led her to write a pioneering book on sex called *Married Love* (1918). She remarried in the same year and wrote *Wise Parenthood*, advocating contraception. In 1921 she set up Britain's first birth-control clinic at Holloway in London, and this was followed by several more clinics in provincial cities. She had a son in 1924 and wrote two further books, *Radiant Motherhood* and *Enduring Passion*.

Margaret THATCHER, born Roberts (1925–). Politician. Born in Grantham, Lincs, the daughter of a grocer, she went to a girls' grammar school and read Chemistry at Oxford. She worked as a research chemist and was an active member of the Conservative party, standing unsuccessfully for Parliament in 1949. She married businessman Denis Thatcher in 1951 and began studying law. She took the Bar Finals in 1953, the same year as she became the mother of twins. Elected Conservative MP for Finchley in 1959, she was made Minister of Education in 1970 and leader of the party in 1975. From 1979 to 1990 she was Britain's first woman Prime Minister.

Glossary

black-out   wartime system of covering windows and switching off outside lights to prevent attack by enemy planes

(the) Blitz   intensive bombing of British cities by German planes

capricious   inconstant, guided by whim

citizen   a person who has full legal and political rights in the country in which they live

class divisions   system by which people are classified according to their economic and social status. Thus the **working** or **labouring** class consists of manual workers in factories, etc., and the **middle class** of professional people, shopkeepers, etc.

Co-op   shop selling groceries, drapery and other goods, run by the Co-operative Society. Founded in Rochdale, Lancashire, in 1844, the Society gave members – in effect all customers – a share in its profits. Before the war the local Co-op was often the biggest shop in many towns, especially in the North of England, and it is still an important retail outlet today.

denizen an inhabitant of a country who does not have full legal or political rights. (Compare with **citizen**.)

(the) Depression   term used to describe the social and economic

conditions prevalent in the 1930s when industries closed and many people were unemployed

elementary school   state-run primary school made non-fee-paying after 1891. Until the advent of the state secondary school in the twentieth century, pupils remained at elementary school until they left to go out to work.

fait accompli   French phrase meaning something already achieved

franchise   right to vote at public elections, especially parliamentary elections

furore   an uproar, usually signifying rage

grammar school   an old-established secondary school with high academic standards, usually fee-paying until the 1944 Education Act, but with some free scholarship places. State secondary schools, for a similar age group, were established in 1902 and run by local authorities.

impotent   unable to perform sexual functions

lobbying   the practice of visiting MPs to persuade them to support a cause

ordination   the receiving of holy orders, enabling a person to become a priest or minister in a church

paedophilia   the condition (in adults) of being sexually attracted to children

prestigious   having high status, impressive

radical   a politician advocating fundamental changes

red box   case containing government papers, which ministers take home with them to work on

Royal Commission   a body of people appointed by the government to investigate and report on a particular issue

socialism   political creed advocating common ownership of the means of production and distribution (land, industry, transport, etc.) and equal rights in a democratic society

suffrage   the right to vote in political elections

suffragist   someone who believes in an extension of the **suffrage**. From the second half of the nineteenth century the term was generally understood to mean someone who wanted to extend the vote to women.

venereal disease (VD)   sexually transmitted diseases such as gonorrhoea and syphilis, which in the nineteenth and early twentieth centuries often led to death

(the) Welfare State   system by which the government takes responsibility for the well-being of its **citizens**, especially the sick, the elderly and the unemployed

Further Reading

General Histories

Ruth Adam, *A Woman's Place 1910–1975*, Chatto & Windus (1975)
Carol Adams, *Ordinary Lives: A Hundred Years Ago*, Virago (1982)
Deirdre Beddoe, *Discovering Women's History*, Pandora Press (1983)
Olivia Bennett, *The Changing Status of Women*, Bell & Hyman (1987)
Angela Holdsworth, *Out of the Doll's House: The Story of Women in the Twentieth Century*, BBC Books (1988)

Special Subjects

Morag Alexander, *A Woman's Place? People, Politics and Power*, Wayland (1983)
Diane Atkinson, *Votes for Women*, Cambridge University Press (1988)
Sarah Boston, *Women Workers and the Trade Unions*, Lawrence & Wishart (1987)
Frank Dawes, *Not in Front of the Servants*, Century Hutchinson (1973)
Celia Fremlin, *War Factory – Mass Observation*, The Cresset Library (1987)
Betty Friedan, *The Feminine Mystique*, Penguin (1963, reprinted 1992)
Germaine Greer, *The Female Eunuch*, Granada (1970)
Pat Hodgson, *Women and Health*, Batsford (1991)

Betty Jerman, *The Lively-Minded Women*, Heinemann (1981)
Ann Kramer, *Women and Politics*, Wayland (1988)
Jane Lewis, *Women in Britain since 1945*, Blackwell (1992)
— *Women in England 1870–1950* (1984)
Caroline Lang, *Keep Smiling Through: Women in the Second World War*, Cambridge University Press (1989)
Jill Liddington and Jill Norris, *One Hand Tied Behind Us – The Rise of the Women's Suffrage Movement*, Virago (1978)
Raynes Minns, *Bombers and Mash*, Virago (1980)
Marguerite Patten, *We'll Eat Again*, Hamlyn/Imperial War Museum (1985)
Joan Perkin, *Victorian Women*, John Murray (1993)
Melanie Phillips, *The Divided House: Women at Westminster*, Sidgwick & Jackson (1980)
Gill Thomas, *Life on All Fronts: Women in the First World War*, Cambridge University Press (1989)
Carol Twinch, *Women on the Land*, Lutterworth Press (1990)
Betty Williams, *Women at Work*, Batsford (1991)

Women's Lives

Daphne Bennett, *Emily Davies and the Liberation of Women*, André Deutsch (1990)
Olivia Bennett, *Annie Besant*, Hamish Hamilton (1988)
Barbara Castle, *Sylvia and Christabel Pankhurst*, Penguin (1987)
Mary Chamberlain, *Growing Up in Lambeth*, Virago (1989)
Rosemary Dinnage, *Annie Besant*, Penguin (1986)
Margaret Forster, *Significant Sisters*, Secker and Warburg (1984)
Valerie Grove, *The Compleat Woman. Marriage, Motherhood, Career: Can She Have It All?*, The Hogarth Press (1988)
Ruth Hall, *Marie Stopes*, André Deutsch (1977)
Josephine Kamm, *How Different From Us: A Biography of Miss Buss and Miss Beale*, Bodley Head (1958)
Hannah Mitchell, *The Hard Way Up*, Virago (1977)
Emmeline Pankhurst, *My Own Story*, Virago (first published 1914, reprinted 1979)
Elizabeth Roberts, *A Woman's Place: An Oral History of Working-Class Women 1890–1940*, Blackwell (1984)
June Rose, *Marie Stopes and the Sexual Revolution*, Faber & Faber (1992)
Mary Stott, *Forgetting's No Excuse*, Faber & Faber (1973)
Dorothy Thompson, *Queen Victoria: Gender and Power*, Virago (1990)
Betty D. Vernon, *Ellen Wilkinson*, Croom Helm (1982)
Mary Wade, *To the Miner Born*, Oriel Press (1984)

Acknowledgements

The author would like to thank the Fawcett Library, London Guildhall University, for the use of their resources. Crown copyright material in the Public Record Office is reproduced by permission of Her Majesty's Stationery Office.

The illustrations are reproduced by kind permission of the following: Hulton Deutsch Collection Ltd, pp. 3, 11, 14, 22, 27, 32–3, 39, 42; the Tate Gallery, p. 5; the National Portrait Gallery, p. 6; Mary Evans Picture Library, pp. 7, 8, 10, 18, 21; Manchester City Art Galleries/Bridgeman Art Library, London, p. 12; e.t. archive, pp. 16–17, 24, 29; Imperial War Museum, pp. 26–7, 35; Rex Features, p. 36; the Estate of Mel Calman, p. 38; Network Photographers/Mayer, pp. 40–1; the Press Association/Barry Batchelor, p. 43.

The front cover shows (top) suffragettes celebrating the release of Mary Leigh from Holloway prison, 1908 (e.t. archive), and (below) women MPs Clare Short and Christine Jackson, 1992 (Kayte Brimacombe/Network).

Changing Britain series editors: Alan Evans and Michael Rawcliffe.

Page numbers in **bold type** also refer to illustrations